Streams
OF Joy

MEDITATIONS ON THE WORTHY LIFE

BARBOUR
PUBLISHING

© 2012 by Barbour Publishing, Inc.

Compiled by Jennifer Hahn.

Print ISBN 978-1-62029-181-8

eBook Editions:
Adobe Digital Edition (.epub) 978-1-62029-642-4
Kindle and MobiPocket Edition (.prc) 978-1-62029-641-7

Published by Barbour Publishing, Inc., P.O. Box 719,
Uhrichsville, Ohio 44683, www.barbourbooks.com

*Our mission is to publish and distribute inspirational products
offering exceptional value and biblical encouragement to the masses.*

Member of the
Evangelical Christian
Publishers Association

Printed in the United States of America.

CONTENTS

Joy in Time and Seasons

&

To every thing there is a season,
and a time to every purpose under the heaven.

ECCLESIASTES 3:1

God's Calendar

William A. Quale

*And God said, Let there be lights in the firmament of
the heaven to divide the day from the night; and let them
be for signs, and for seasons, and for days, and years.*

Genesis 1:14

*H*ours and minutes are man's invention. Weeks and
days and nights and the month and the year are God's
inventions. A seventh day for rest God said, and the
week was put in the calendar.

One day light and one dark, and the day was
created. One advent and exit of the silvery moon, and
the month was included in its silvery circuit. The planet's
panting journey around the sun, and the year became a
terrestrial and celestial fact. Twelve comings and goings
of the moon, with a few days excess thrown in for good
measure, as is customary with God; and God's calendar
is an accomplished loveliness.

In His Time
R.T. Kendall

He chose to be mistreated along with the people of
God rather than to enjoy the fleeting pleasures of sin.

Hebrews 11:25 NIV

*W*hen God shows us that he is going to use us (and
he can do that), we usually tend to think that we are
going to see this happen in the next week or two. What
often happens is that it is a long time before God gets
around to using us as He has planned. Take Moses.
When Moses grew up, he refused to be called the son of
Pharaoh's daughter, "choosing rather to suffer affliction
with the people of God, than to enjoy the pleasures of
sin for a season" (Hebrews 11:25). Moses thought that
when he left the palace and identified himself with his
brethren, they would clap their hands and say, "Welcome.
We've been waiting for you to come." The truth is they
rejected him, and Moses needed another forty years of
preparation.

It may be a good while indeed before God's greater
purpose in us will be realized. It could be that you, too, are
in a similar situation. Perhaps you are older and you have
yet to see what God's greater purpose in your own life is.
Perhaps you have just about given up. You thought at one
time that God was going to use you. You were convinced
of it. God's message to you right now is: the end is not yet.

GOD'S TIMING

Mrs. Charles E. Cowman

By faith Moses. . .
choosing rather to suffer. . .
HEBREWS 11:24–25

*B*y faith Moses refused. Faith rests on promise; to faith the promise is equivalent to fulfillment; and if only we have the one, we may dare to count on the other as already ours. It matters comparatively little that the thing promised is not given; it is sure and certain because God has pledged His word for it, and in anticipation we may enter on its enjoyment. Had Moses simply acted on what he saw, he had never left Pharaoh's palace.

Evidently God's time had not arrived, nor could it come until the heat of his spirit had slowly evaporated in the desert air and he had learned the hardest of all lessons, that "by strength shall no man prevail."

Faith is only possible when we are on God's plan and stand on God's promise. It is useless to pray for increased faith until we have fulfilled the conditions of faith. It is useless to waste time on regrets and tears over the failures which are due to our unbelief.

Ascertain your place in God's plan, and get on to it. Feed on God's promises. When each of these conditions is realized, faith comes of itself, and there is absolutely nothing which is impossible. The believing souls will then be as the metal track along which God travels to men in love, grace, and truth.

CROWDING OUR GOD

John Henry Jowett

*"Only take heed to thyself, and keep thy soul diligently,
lest thou forget the things which thine eyes have seen,
and lest they depart from thy heart. . . ."*

DEUTERONOMY 4:9

We may oppose a man and hinder him in his work, or we may directly injure him, or we may ignore him and treat him as nothing. Or we may forget him! Opposition, injury, contempt, neglect, forgetfulness! Surely this is a descending scale, and the last is the worst. And yet we can forget the Lord God. We can forget all His benefits. We can easily put Him out of mind.

What shall we do to escape this great disaster? "Take heed to thyself!" To take heed is to be at the helm and not asleep in the cabin. It is to steer and not to drift. It is to keep our eyes on the compass and our hands on the wheel. It is to know where we are going. We never deliberately forget our Lord; we carelessly drift into it. "Take heed."

"And keep thy soul diligently." Gardens run to seed, and ill weeds grow apace. The fair things are crowded out, and the weed reigns everywhere. It is ever so with my soul. If I neglect it, the flowers of holy desire and devotion will be choked by weeds of worldliness. God will be crowded out, and the garden of the soul will become a wilderness of neglect and sin.

REST IN THE LORD

from *Daily Strength for Daily Needs*

*The LORD shall give thee rest from thy sorrow, and from thy fear,
and from the hard bondage wherein thou wast made to serve.*

ISAIAH 14:3

*Today, beneath Thy chastening eye, I crave alone for peace and rest;
submissive in Thy hand to lie, and feel that it is best.*

J. G. WHITTIER

*O Lord, who are as the Shadow of a great Rock in a weary
land, who beholdest Thy weak creatures weary of labour,
weary of pleasure, weary of hope deferred, weary of self;
in Thine abundant compassion and unutterable tenderness,
bring us, I pray Thee, unto Thy rest. Amen.*

CHRISTINA G. ROSSETTI

*Grant to me above all things that can be desired, to rest in Thee,
and in Thee to have my heart at peace. Thou art the true peace
of the heart, Thou its only rest; out of Thee all things are hard
and restless. In this very peace, that is, in Thee, the One
Chiefest Eternal Good, I will sleep and rest. Amen.*

THOMAS Á KEMPIS

*Thou hast made us for Thyself, O Lord;
and our heart is restless until it rests in Thee.*

ST. AUGUSTINE

THE DAY STAR

T. C. Horton and Charles E. Hurlburt

*We also have the prophetic message as something completely
reliable, and you will do well to pay attention to it,
as to a light shining in a dark place, until the day
dawns and the morning star rises in your hearts.*

2 PETER 1:19 NIV

In the Gospel of John, we read, "In Him was life; and
the life was the light of men." We have the sure Word of
God. It is a lamp to our feet and a light unto our path.
Our hearts are darkened by the evil nature within us, but
when Jesus comes into our hearts He illumines the Word
of God and shines with all the effulgence of His glory.
Perpetual day is for those who walk in His light. Every
day is a good day, and the eternal glory awaits us.

Blessed Lord, our Light, shine in our hearts and
lives this day, and may we reflect Thy glory. Amen.

DAY BY DAY

Andrew Murray

And the people shall go out and
gather a certain rate every day. . . .

EXODUS 16:4

𝒯he day's portion in its day: such was the rule for God's
giving and man's working in the gathering of the manna.
It is still the law in all the dealings of God's grace
with His children. A clear insight into the beauty and
application of this arrangement is a wonderful help in
understanding how one, who feels himself utterly weak,
can have the confidence and the perseverance to hold
on brightly through all the years of his earthly course. A
doctor was once asked by a patient who had met with
a serious accident: "Doctor, how long shall I have to lie
here?" The answer, "Only a day at a time," taught the
patient a precious lesson. It was the same lesson God had
recorded for His people of all ages long before: The day's
portion in its day.

RECKONING UP THINGS

John Henry Jowett

Teach us to number our days,
that we may gain a heart of wisdom.

PSALM 90:12 NIV

*N*umbering things is one of the healthful exercises of the spiritual life. Unless we count, memory is apt to be very tricky and to snare us into strange forgetfulness. Unless we count what we have given away, we are very apt to exaggerate our bounty. We often think we have given when we have only listened to appeals; the mere audience has been mistaken for active beneficence. The remedy for all this is occasionally to count our benevolence and see how we stand in a balance-sheet which we could present to the Lord Himself.

And we must count our blessings. It is when our arithmetic fails in the task, and when counting God's blessings is like telling the number of the stars, that our souls bow low before the eternal goodness, and all murmuring dies away like cloud-spots in the dawn.

And we must also "number our days." We are wasteful with them, and we throw them away as though they are ours in endless procession. And yet there are only seven days in a week! A day is of immeasurable preciousness, for what high accomplishment may it not witness? A day in health or in sickness, spent unto God and applied unto wisdom, will gather treasures more precious than rubies and gold.

Can You Be Holy?

Ken Abraham

Be ye holy in all manner of conversation;
Because it is written, Be ye holy; for I am holy. . . .
Pass the time of your sojourning here in fear.

1 PETER 1:15–17

*B*elieve that God can make you holy here and now.
Many devout Christians hope to become holy someday,
if not here on earth, hopefully in heaven. But the Spirit
of God impressed Peter in those first few years after
Pentecost to exhort us: "Be holy yourselves also in all
your behavior; because it is written, 'You shall be holy,
for I am holy.' Clearly, Peter is implying that holiness is
something to be pursued in this lifetime, not simply in
the life to come.

God can deliver you from the bondage of sin. He
can cleanse your heart, mind, and mouth; and He can fill
you with His Holy Presence—right now.

THE GREATNESS OF DOING

Brother Lawrence

And as for you, brothers and sisters,
never tire of doing what is good.

2 THESSALONIANS 3:13 NIV

That we ought, once and for all, heartily to put our whole trust in God and make a total surrender of ourselves to Him, secure that He would not deceive us.

That we ought not to be weary of doing little things for the love of God, who regards not the greatness of the work but the love with which it is performed. That we should not wonder if, in the beginning, we often failed in our endeavors, but that at last we should gain a habit, which will naturally produce its acts in us, without our care, and to our exceeding great delight.

DAILY BREAD

from *Daily Strength for Daily Needs*

Thou openest thine hand,
and satisfiest the desire of every living thing.

PSALM 145:16

What Thou shalt to-day provide,
Let me as a child receive;
What to-morrow may betide,
Calmly to Thy wisdom leave.
'Tis enough that thou wilt care;
Why should I the burden bear?

JOHN NEWTON

*H*ave we found that anxiety about possible consequences increased the clearness of our judgment, made us wiser and braver in meeting the present, and armed ourselves for the future? . . . If we had prayed for this day's bread and left the next to itself, if we had not huddled our days together, not allotting to each its appointed task, but ever deferring that to the future and drawing upon the future for its own troubles, which must be met when they come whether we have anticipated them or not, we should have found a simplicity and honesty in our lives, a capacity for work, an enjoyment in it, to which we are now, for the most part, strangers.

F. D. MAURICE

Sail On!

Mrs. Charles E. Cowman

Hitherto hath the LORD helped us.
1 SAMUEL 7:12

So now into another year we sail, and something of what we may expect as we continue our voyage we may infer from the past. Without doubt, storms will come as they came in the bygone days. But we will give them firm and courageous welcome, for we have already weathered so many storms that we are unafraid of the wind and the tide, the lightning and the snow.

And so we shall—when the Voyage is completed—drop anchor where no storms come, but where the green swell is at last in the haven dumb, and we are forever out of the swing of the Sea.

We have come very safely—hitherto;
And sometimes seas were calm, and skies were blue;
Sometimes the wild waves rose—the tempest roared;
But never barque went down with Christ on board.
And so it shall be to the very end—
Through ebb or flow, the one unchanging Friend,
Ruling the waves which sink at His command,
Holding them in the hollow in His hand.
There comes an hour, when, every tempest o'er
The harbour lights are reached, the golden shores:
Never, oh nevermore to fret or fear—
Christ, give us faith to praise Thee even here!

MARY GORGES

DAY BY DAY

from *Daily Strength for Daily Needs*

*The king's officials answered him, "Your servants are
ready to do whatever our lord the king chooses."*

2 SAMUEL 15:15 NIV

*I*f we are really and always and equally ready to do
whatsoever the King appoints, all the trials and vexations
arising from any change in His appointments, great or
small, simply do not exist. If He appoints me to work
there, shall I lament that I am not to work here? If He
appoints me to wait indoors today, am I to be annoyed
because I am not to work out-of-doors? If I meant to
write His messages this morning, shall I grumble because
He sends interrupting visitors, rich or poor, to whom
I am to speak them, or show kindness for His sake, or
at least obey His command, Be courteous? If all my
members are really at His disposal, why should I be put
out if today's appointment is some simple work for my
hands or errands for my feet, instead of some seemingly
more important doing of head or tongue?

TIME WITH GOD

Andrew Murray

For this shall every one that is godly pray unto
thee in a time when thou mayest be found. . . .

PSALM 32:6

*O*my God! I do believe in Thee. I believe in Thee as
the Father, Infinite in Thy Love and Power. And as the
Son, my Redeemer and my Life. And as the Holy Spirit,
Comforter and Guide and Strength. Three-in-One God,
I have faith in Thee. I know and am sure that all that
Thou art to me, that all Thou hast promised Thou wilt
perform.

Lord Jesus, increase this faith! Teach me to take
time and wait and worship in the Holy Presence until
my faith takes in all there is in my God for me. Let it see
Him as the Fountain of all Life, working with Almighty
Strength to accomplish His will in the world and in me.
Let it see Him in His Love longing to meet and fulfill
my desires. Let it so take possession of my heart and
life that through faith God alone may dwell there. Lord
Jesus, help me! With my whole heart would I believe in
God. Let faith in God each moment fill me.

THE REST OF GOD

D. L. Moody

*"Come to me, all you who are weary and burdened,
and I will give you rest."*

MATTHEW 11:28 NIV

A mother had a child that was sick. One day the doctor came in and said that the symptoms were very unfavorable. He took the mother out of the room and told her that the child could not live. The mother went into the room where the child lay and began to talk to the child and tried to divert its mind.

"Darling, do you know you will soon hear the music of heaven?"

And the child turned its head away and said, "Oh, mamma, I am so tired and so sick that I think it would make me worse to hear all that music."

"Well," the mother said, "you will soon see Jesus. You will see the seraphim and cherubim and the streets all paved with gold," and she went on picturing heaven as it is described in Revelation.

The child again turned its head and said, "Oh, mamma, I am so tired that I think it would make me worse to see all those beautiful things!"

The mother took the child up in her arms and pressed her to her loving heart. And the little sick one whispered, "If Jesus will only take me in His arms and let me rest!"

Dear friend, are you not tired and weary of sin? Are you not weary of the turmoil of life? You can find rest on the bosom of the Son of God.

GOD PROVIDES FOR OUR TOMORROW

from *Daily Strength for Daily Needs*

*Take no thought for your life, what ye shall eat, or what ye
shall drink, nor yet for your body, what ye shall put on.*

MATTHEW 6:25

*I*t has been well said that no man ever sank under the
burden of the day. It is when tomorrow's burden is added
to the burden of today that the weight is more than a
man can bear. Never load yourselves so, my friends. If
you find yourselves so loaded, at least remember this: It
is your own doing, not God's. He begs you to leave the
future to Him, and mind the present.

GEORGE MACDONALD

Showers upon the Earth

T. C. Horton and Charles E. Hurlburt

May he be like rain falling on a mown field,
like showers watering the earth.

PSALM 72:6 NIV

*O*ur lives grow dusty, dry, and desert in our earthly pilgrimage, but He who seeks a love that is fresh and pure and strong comes down upon us as "The Showers Upon The Earth." Have you turned to Him today and found that cool, refreshing, cleansing blessing which He seeks to give?

There shall be showers of blessing,
Oh, that today they might fall!
Now, as to God we're confessing,
Now, as on Jesus we call.

CHRISTMAS CHEER
John Henry Jowett

. . .good will toward men. . .
LUKE 2:14

*T*he heavens are not filled with hostility. The sky does not express a frown. When I look up I do not contemplate a face of brass but the face of infinite goodwill. Yet when I was a child, many a picture has made me think of God as suspicious, inhumanly watchful, always looking round the corner to catch me at the fall. That "eye," placed in the sky of many a picture and placed there to represent God, filled my heart with a chilling fear. That God was to me a magnified policeman, watching for wrongdoers and ever ready for the infliction of punishment. It was all a frightful perversion of the gracious teaching of Jesus.

Heaven overflows with goodwill toward men! Our God not only wishes good, He wills it! "He gave His only begotten Son," as the sacred expression of His infinite good will. He has goodwill toward thee and me, and mine and thine. Let that holy thought make our Christmas cheer.

THE CHRIST OF CHRISTMAS

William A. Quale

"Very truly I tell you, you will weep and mourn while the world rejoices. You will grieve, but your grief will turn to joy."

JOHN 16:20 NIV

*B*efore Christ came, it was only a month of icy winter fierce in onset of frost and snow and raging icy wind, but since his coming, December, however angry its beginning, its ending has always been in a burst of laughter. When December is at its frozen noon, all of a sudden mirth invades this spacious winter and voice of man and woman, youth and maid, schoolboy and little toddling child, leaps to a song, and the icy church bells sing a carol and Christmas chimneys have radiant light. People forget their weeping or are ashamed to invade Christmas with their tears. December has been silenced of his boisterous anger by the more boisterous good nature of the whole world of happy hearts.

December himself learns a Christmas tune and sings with tempestuous mirth a melody, the burden of which I catch to be: "Merry Christmas, Peace on earth, goodwill to men. Christ is come and has changed my winter into laughing spring. I am less December now than June. My flowers are children's smiling faces and my birds' singing is the Christmas laughter of such hearts as have heard that in Bethlehem a child is born and the angels sing and I, December of the frozen heart, have caught the angels' tune, Praise! Praise!"

Joy in Increasing Our Faith

As for God, his way is perfect: The LORD's word is flawless; he shields all who take refuge in him.

PSALM 18:30 NIV

The Unknown Journey

John Henry Jowett

He went out, not knowing whither he went.

HEBREWS 11:8

Abram began his journey without any knowledge of his ultimate destination. He obeyed a noble impulse without any discernment of its consequences. He took "one step," and he did not "ask to see the distant scene." And that is faith, to do God's will here and now, quietly leaving the results to Him. Faith is not concerned with the entire chain; its devoted attention is fixed upon the immediate link. Faith is not knowledge of a moral process; it is fidelity in a moral act. Faith leaves something to the Lord; it obeys His immediate commandment and leaves to Him direction and destiny.

And so faith is accompanied by serenity. "He that believeth shall not make haste"—or, more literally, "shall not get into a fuss." He shall not get into a panic, neither fetching fears from his yesterdays nor from his tomorrows. Concerning his yesterdays Faith says, "Thou hast beset me behind." Concerning his tomorrows Faith says, "Thou hast beset me before." Concerning his today Faith says, "Thou hast laid Thine hand upon me." That is enough, just to feel the pressure of the guiding hand.

From Little Faith
to Great Faith

Charles H. Spurgeon

Have faith in God.
MARK 11:22

*F*aith is the foot of the soul by which it can march along the road of the commandments. . . . Faith is the oil enabling the wheels of holy devotion and of earnest piety to move well; and without faith the wheels are taken from the chariot, and we drag heavily. With faith I can do all things; without faith I shall neither have the inclination nor the power to do anything in the service of God. If you would find the men who serve God the best, you must look for the men of the most faith. Little faith will save a man, but little faith cannot defeat things for God. Would you be comfortable and happy? Would you enjoy religion? Would you have the religion of cheerfulness and not that of gloom? Then "have faith in God." If you love darkness and are satisfied to dwell in gloom and misery, then be content with little faith; but if you love the sunshine and would sing songs of rejoicing, covet earnestly this best gift, "great faith."

TRUST
Jill Briscoe

Christ in you, the hope of glory.
COLOSSIANS 1:27

*T*he king of Hearts in the book of Proverbs trusted his queen. So would our King of Hearts in heaven trust us! This is what really blows my mind. God trusts us! Yes, He does. He trusts us to come through for Him. He looks to us. Think about it for a minute. He trusts us with the Holy Spirit. He has not only sent His Spirit into our hearts crying, "Abba, Father," He has sent Him knowing our hearts are unholy. He trusts us then to be obedient to His holy promptings and hate the sin He hates, and repent of the selfishness He abhors. He trusts us to clean our spiritual house, just as diligently as the Proverbs woman cleaned her physical house.

Not only does our King of Hearts trust us with His Spirit, He trusts us with His Son! He trusts us to bid Him welcome, make Him feel at home, and settle Him down. Paul prayed the strangest prayer one day. He prayed for some new converts that "Christ may dwell in your hearts by faith. . ." (Ephesians 3:17). Was not Christ already dwelling in their hearts? Surely, but the secret lies on the word that the apostle used—the word *dwell*. The meaning is clear in the original language. It means to "settle down and feel at home."

The Communion of Faith

Brother Lawrence

*That you, being rooted and established in love, may have power,
together with all the Lord's holy people, to grasp how wide
and long and high and deep is the love of Christ, and to know
this love that surpasses knowledge—that you may be filled
to the measure of all the fullness of God.*

EPHESIANS 3:17–19 NIV

𝒯he elevating and perfecting of character comes largely
through sorrow. This is the "mystery of the Cross." All
process is by crucifixion. Experiences sad and dark,
seemingly cruel, press upon us. The past is tear-worn
and furrowed, and the future glooms with shapes of
trial. Like Paul, we "know not what shall befall us there."
Only the Holy Spirit witnessed to him, and experience
witnesses to us, that "afflictions abide" us. I murmured
at this, until I saw the crosses and stakes and racks and
scaffolds of all ages, and the white feet of those who
made these the stairways up which they climbed to light,
to truth, to God. Light breaks when I see Jesus, scarred
with whipping, thorn-crowned, staggering up Calvary
beneath His Cross. I falter sometimes when I try to say,
"It is good for me that I have been afflicted." But I can
now and then catch a glimpse of the truth of it, when
the light of some suffering and conquering hero breaks
through the blinding mist of my tears. Gethsemanes
have deeper and grander meanings than Canas.

ALL:
OR NOTHING AT ALL

Andrew Murray

"Yield yourselves unto God, as those that are alive from the dead, and your members as instruments of righteousness unto God."

ROMANS 6:13

The cause of the weakness of your Christian life is that you want to work it out partly, and to let God help you. And that cannot be. You must come to be utterly helpless, to let God work, and God will work gloriously. It is this that we need if we are indeed to be workers for God. I could go through scripture and prove to you how Moses, when he led Israel out of Egypt; how Joshua, when he brought them into the land of Canaan; how all God's servants in the Old Testament counted upon the omnipotence of God doing impossibilities. And this God lives today, and this God is the God of every child of His. And yet we are some of us wanting God to give us a little help while we do our best, instead of coming to understand what God wants, and to say: I can do nothing, God must and will do all. Have you said: In worship, in work, in sanctification, in obedience to God, I can do nothing of myself, and so my place is to worship the omnipotent God and to believe that He will work in me every moment. Oh, may God teach us this!

STAND STILL

Charles H. Spurgeon

*"Stand firm and you will see the deliverance
the LORD will bring you today."*

EXODUS 14:13 NIV

*T*hese words contain God's command to the believer
when he is reduced to great straits and brought into
extraordinary difficulties. He cannot retreat; he cannot
go forward; he is shut up on the right hand and on the
left; what is he now to do? The Master's word to him is,
"Stand still."

Despair whispers, "Lie down and die; give it all up."
Cowardice says, "Retreat; go back to the world's way
of action; you cannot play the Christian's part, it is too
difficult." But however much Satan may argue this course
upon you, you cannot follow it if you are a child of God.
His divine fiat has bid thee go from strength to strength,
and so thou shalt, and neither death nor hell shall turn
thee from thy course. Precipitancy cries, "Do something.
Stir yourself; to stand still and wait is sheer idleness." We
must be doing something at once—we must do it, so we
think—instead of loosing it to the Lord, who will not
only do something but will do everything. Presumption
boasts, "If the sea be before you, march into it and expect
a miracle." But Faith listens neither to Presumption, nor
to Despair, nor to Cowardice, nor to Precipitancy, but it
hears God say, "Stand still," and immoveable as a rock it
stands.

THE SHOUT OF FAITH
Hannah Whitall Smith

*And it came to pass, when. . .the people shouted
with a great shout, that the wall fell down flat.*

JOSHUA 6:20

*T*he walls may look as high and as immovable as ever,
and prudence may say it is not safe to shout until the
victory is actually won. But the faith that can shout in
the midst of the sorest stress of temptation, "Jesus saves
me; He saves me now!" such a faith will be sure to win
a glorious and a speedy victory. Many of God's children
have tried this plan and have found it to work far beyond even their expectations. Temptations have come
in upon them like a flood, temptations to irritability
or to wicked thoughts or to bitterness of spirit or to
a thousand other things, and they have seen their
danger; and their fears and their feelings have declared
that there was no hope of escape. But their faith has
laid hold of this grand fact that Christ has conquered,
and they have fixed their gaze on the unseen power of
God's salvation and have given their shout of victory,
"The Lord saves! He saves me now! I am more than
conqueror through Him that loves me!" And the result
is always a glorious victory.

Assurance of Faith
D. L. Moody

The eternal God is thy refuge, and underneath are the
everlasting arms: and he shall thrust out the enemy from
before thee; and shall say, Destroy them.

DEUTERONOMY 33:27

I was standing with a friend at his garden gate one evening when two little children came by. As they approached us he said to me, "Watch the difference in these two boys." Taking one of them in his arms, he stood him on the gatepost, and stepping back a few feet, he folded his arms and called to the little fellow to jump. In an instant the boy sprang toward him and was caught in his arms. Then turning to the second boy, he tried the same experiment. But in the second case it was different. The child trembled and refused to move. My friend held out his arms and tried to induce the child to trust to his strength, but nothing could move him. At last my friend had to lift him down from the post and let him go.

"What makes such a difference in the two?" I asked. My friend smiled and said, "The first is my own boy and knows me, but the other is a stranger's child whom I have never seen before."

So it is with us. We hesitate to trust ourselves to the loving One whose plans for us are far higher than any we have ourselves made. He, too, with outstretched arms, calls us.

CHRIST JESUS: THE END

Brother Lawrence

*"For in him we live and move
and have our being. . . ."*

ACTS 17:28 NIV

*I*t is, however, necessary to put our whole trust in God,
laying aside all other cares and even some particular
forms of devotion, though very good in themselves, yet
such as one often engages is unreasonable, because these
devotions are only a means to attain the end. So when
by this exercise of the presence of God we are with Him
who is our end, it is then useless to return to the means;
but we may continue with Him our commerce of love,
preserving in His holy presence, by an act of praise, of
adoration, or of desire.

Amazing Grace

Charles H. Spurgeon

"My grace is sufficient for you. . ."
2 Corinthians 12:9 NIV

If none of God's saints were poor and tired, we should not know half so well the consolations of divine grace. When we find the wanderer who has not known where to lay his head, who yet can say, "Still I will trust in the Lord"; when we see the pauper starving on bread and water, who still glories in Jesus; when we see the bereaved widow overwhelmed in affliction, and yet having faith in Christ, oh! what honor it reflects on the gospel. Saints bear up under every discouragement, believing that all things work together for their good, and that out of apparent evils a real blessing shall ultimately spring— that their God will either work a deliverance for them speedily or most assuredly support them in the trouble, as long as He is pleased to keep them in it. This patience of the saints proves the power of divine grace. There is a lighthouse out at sea; it is a calm night—I cannot tell whether the edifice is firm; the tempest must rage about it, and then I shall know whether it will stand.

If then, yours be a much-tried path, rejoice in it, because you will better show forth the all-sufficient grace of God. As for His failing you, never dream of it—hate the thought. The God who has been sufficient until now should be trusted to the end.

Little Faith: Big Promise

Andrew Murray

If ye have faith as a grain of mustard seed. . .
nothing shall be impossible unto you.

Matthew 17:20

*D*isciples of Jesus! who have asked the Master to teach you to pray, come now and accept His lessons. He tells you that prayer is the path to faith, strong faith, that can cast out devils. He tells you, "If ye have faith, nothing shall be impossible unto you"; let this glorious promise encourage you to pray much. Is the prize not worth the price? Shall we not give up all to follow Jesus in the path He opens to us here; shall we not, if need be, fast? Shall we not do anything that neither the body nor the world around hinder us in our great life-work— having intercourse with our God in prayer—that we may become men of faith, whom He can use in His work of saving the world?

God's Blank Checkbook
Mrs. Charles E. Cowman

I AM THAT I AM...
EXODUS 3:14

God gave Moses a blank check, and as life went forward for the next forty years, Moses kept filling in the blank with his special need. He filled in fearlessness before Pharaoh. He filled in guidance across the Red Sea. He filled in manna for the whole population. He filled in water from the rock. He filled in guidance through the wilderness. He filled in victory over Amalek. He filled in clear revelation at Sinai. And so Moses, for the rest of his life, had little else to do than to go quietly alone, and taking God's blank checkbook, signed by God's name, I am that I am, wrote in I am guidance; I am bread. He presented the check and God honored it. And whenever you come to live upon God's plan as Moses from that moment did, you may absolutely trust God. And when you come down to the end you will say, "Not one thing hath failed of all the good things which the LORD your God spake concerning you" (Joshua 23:14).

A. B. SIMPSON

Enduring Faith

Ken Abraham

Know therefore that the Lord thy God, he is God, the faithful God, which keepeth covenant and mercy with them that love him and keep his commandments to a thousand generations.

Deuteronomy 7:9

If God has placed a dream in your heart, do not give up. Be diligent. Endure even in the dungeons of life. Our generation knows little about endurance; we are so accustomed to instant gratification. Endurance does not mean, "I'll just hang in there until Jesus comes." Endurance means, "I believe that what God said He would do, He will, in fact, do!" Endurance means that you can say with the ancient prophet Habakkuk, "Although the fig tree shall not blossom, neither shall fruit be in the vines; the labor of the olive shall fail, and the fields shall yield no meat; the flock shall be cut off from the fold, and there shall be no herd in the stalls: Yet I will rejoice in the Lord, I will joy in the God of my salvation. The Lord God is my strength, and he will make my feet like hinds' feet, and he will make me to walk upon mine high places" (Habakkuk 3:17–19).

That is what endurance is all about!

Your days of preparation may even now be nearing an end. The delay you have endured has not been an accident but was according to His plan and for His purposes.

"CAN GOD?"

Mrs. Charles E. Cowman

They spoke against God; they said,
"Can God really spread a table in the wilderness?"

PSALM 78:19 NIV

*C*an God?" Oh, fatal question! It shut Israel out of the land of Promise. And we are in danger of making the same mistake. Can God find me a situation or provide food for my children? Can God keep me from yielding to that besetting sin? Can God extricate me from this terrible snare in which I am entangled? We look at the difficulties, the surges that are rolling high, and we say, "If Thou canst do anything, help us!"

They said, "Can God?" It hurt and wounded God deeply. Say no more, "Can God?" Rather say this, "God Can!" That will clear up many a problem. That will bring you through many a difficulty in your life. There is no strength in unbelief.

Has the life of God's people reached the utmost limit of what God can do for them? Surely not! God has new places and new developments and new resources. He can do new things, unheard-of hidden things, hidden things! Let us enlarge our hearts and not limit Him.

We must desire and believe. We must ask and expect that God will do unlooked-for things! We must set our faith on a God of whom men do not know what He hath prepared for them that wait for Him.

ANDREW MURRAY

FORGOTTEN IN PLENTY, REMEMBERED IN POVERTY

Jill Briscoe

"Give, and it will be given to you. A good measure, pressed down, shaken together and running over, will be poured into your lap. . . ."

LUKE 6:38 NIV

*W*hat do you have in the house?" Elisha asked the poor widow.

"Nothing," she replied. . . . "Nothing to sell, nothing to eat, nothing to burn on the fire, nothing to sleep on. . . ."

"Think," the prophet urged. "Are you sure there's nothing in the house?"

"Just a little pot of oil," she replied.

Elisha began to explain what she must do. . . .

Turning to the amazed children who had watched the whole glorious turn of events, their mother began to give them orders. "We are going to reach out to our neighbors," the widow announced. . . . "Run now and ask for empty vessels—get many of them!"

"When you learn to pour yourself out into the empty vessels all around you and lose your own problems in seeking to 'be' the answer to theirs, then you will be able to rejoice in My fullness," Elisha said to the little widow as she busily kept filling vessel after vessel that her sons brought to her.

The little lady laughed. "I'm simply obeying the Word of God, given to me by the man of God, about the provision of God, and I'm learning that the oil flows according to my faith!"

TRUST IN THE LORD

from *Daily Strength for Daily Needs*

*"Trust in the LORD, and do good; so shalt thou
dwell in the land, and verily thou shalt be fed."*

PSALM 37:3

*Build a little fence of trust
Around today;
Fill the space with loving work,
And therein stay;
Look not through the sheltering bars
Upon tomorrow,
God will help thee bear what comes,
Of joy or sorrow.*

MARY FRANCES BUTTS

*L*et us bow our souls and say, "Behold the handmaid
of the Lord!" Let us lift up our hearts and ask, "Lord,
what wouldst thou have me to do?" Then light from the
opened heaven shall stream on our daily task, revealing
the grains of gold, when yesterday all seemed dust; a
hand shall sustain us and our daily burden, so that,
smiling at yesterday's fears, we shall say, "This is easy,
this is light"; every "lion in the way," as we come up to
it, shall be seen chained, and leave open the gates of
the Palace Beautiful; and to us, even to us, feeble and
fluctuating as we are, ministries shall be assigned, and
through our hands blessings shall be conveyed in which
the spirit of just men make perfect might delight.

ELIZABETH CHARLES

THE DEEP

Mrs. Charles E. Cowman

Launch out into the deep.

LUKE 5:4

*H*ow deep He does not say. The depth into which we launch will depend upon how perfectly we have given up the shore, and the greatness of our need, and the apprehension of our possibilities.

We are to launch out into the deep of God's Word, which the Spirit can open up to us in such crystal fathomless meaning that the same words we have accepted in times past will have an ocean meaning in them, which renders their first meaning to us very shallow.

Into the deep of the Father's will, until He becomes a bright, dazzling, sweet, fathomless summer sea, in which we bathe and bask and breathe and lose ourselves and our sorrows in the calmness and peace of His everlasting presence.

Into the deep of the Holy Spirit, until He becomes a bright, marvelous answer to prayer, the most careful and tender guidance, the most thoughtful anticipation of our needs, the most accurate and supernatural shaping of our events.

Into the deep of God's purposes and coming kingdom, until the Lord's coming and His millennial reign are opened up to us; and beyond these the bright entrancing ages on ages unfold themselves, until the mental eye is dazed with light, and the heart flutters with inexpressible anticipations of its joy with Jesus and the glory to be revealed.

TRUSTING IN THE DARKNESS

D. L. Moody

Now faith is the substance of things hoped for,
the evidence of things not seen.

HEBREWS 11:1

Suppose I have a sick boy. I know nothing about medicine, but I call in the doctor and put that boy's life and everything into his hands. I do not fail to believe in him, and I do not interfere at all. Do you call that trusting in the dark? Not at all! I used my best judgment, and I put that boy's life into the hands of a good physician.

You have a soul diseased. Put it into the hand of the Great Physician! Trust Him, and He will take care of it. He has had some of the most hopeless cases. He was able to heal all that came to Him while on earth. He is the same today.

We must trust God in time of trouble, in time of bereavement. You can trust Him with your soul until your dying day, if you will. Will you not do it?

IRRESISTIBLE TRUST

Hannah Whitall Smith

"And I, when I am lifted up from the earth,
will draw all people to myself."

JOHN 12:32 NIV

If you are an uncomfortable Christian, then the only thing to give you a thoroughly comfortable religious life is to know God. The psalmist says that they that know God's name will put their trust in Him, and it is, I am convinced, impossible for anyone really to know Him and not to trust Him. A trustworthy person commands trust, not in the sense of ordering people to trust him, but by irresistibly winning their trust by his trustworthiness.

What our Lord declares is eternally true, "And I, if I be lifted up, will draw all men unto me." When once you know Him, Christ is absolutely irresistible. You can no more help trusting Him than you can help breathing. And could the whole world but know Him as He is, the whole world, sinners and all, would fall at His feet in adoring worship. They simply could not help it. His surpassing loveliness would carry all before it.

How then can we become acquainted with God?

There are two things necessary: First, God must reveal Himself; and second, we must accept His revelation and believe what He reveals.

Joy in Communicating with the Father

*He shall pray unto God, and he will be favourable
unto him: and he shall see his face with joy:
for he will render unto man his righteousness.*

JOB 33:26

THE MODEL PRAYER

Andrew Murray

After this manner therefore pray ye:
Our Father which art in heaven...

MATTHEW 6:9

*E*very teacher knows the power of example. He not only tells the child what to do and how to do it but shows him how it really can be done. In condescension to our weakness, our heavenly Teacher has given us the very words we are to take with us as we draw near to our Father. We have in them a form of prayer in which there breathes the freshness and fullness of the Eternal Life. So simple that the child can lisp it, so divinely rich that it comprehends all that God can give. A form of prayer that becomes the model and inspiration for all other prayer, and yet always draws us back to itself as the deepest utterance of our souls before our God.

"Our Father which art in heaven!" To appreciate this word of adoration aright, I must remember that none of the saints in scripture had ever ventured to address God as their Father.

THE PROMISE-KEEPER

Andrew Murray

Unless I go away, the Advocate will not come to you;
but if I go, I will send him to you.

JOHN 16:7 NIV

*I*n all our prayer let us remember the lesson the Savior would teach us this day, that if there is one thing on earth we can be sure of, it is this, that the Father desires to have us filled with His Spirit, that He delights to give us His Spirit.

And when once we have learned thus to believe for ourselves, and each day to take out of the treasure we hold in heaven, what liberty and power to pray for the outpouring of the Spirit on the Church of God, on all flesh, on individuals, or on special efforts!

He that has once learned to know the Father in prayer for himself, learns to pray most confidently for others, too. The Father gives the Holy Spirit to them that ask Him, not least, but most, when they ask for others.

Lord, teach us to pray.

THE POTENCY OF PRAYER

E. M. Bounds

The righteous cry, and the LORD heareth,
and delivereth them out of all their troubles.

PSALM 34:17

$\mathcal{I}$t was said of the late C. H. Spurgeon that he glided from laughter to prayer with the naturalness of one who lived in both elements. With him the habit of prayer was free and unfettered. He lived in constant fellowship with his Father in heaven. He was ever in touch with God, and thus it was as natural for him to pray as it was for him to breathe.

That is the attitude with regard to prayer that ought to mark every child of God. There are, and there ought to be, stated seasons of communication with God when, everything else is shut out, we come into His presence to talk to Him and to let Him speak to us; and out of such seasons springs that beautiful habit of prayer that weaves a golden bond between earth and heaven.

In every circumstance of life, prayer is the most natural outpouring of the soul, the unhindered turning to God for communion and direction. . . . The heart leaps to meet with God.

TRANSFORMED

Brother Lawrence

Be transformed by the renewing of your mind.

ROMANS 12:2 NIV

As for my set hours of prayer, they are only a continuation of the same exercise. Sometimes I consider myself there as a stone before a carver, whereof he is to make a statue; presenting myself thus before God, I desire Him to form His perfect image in my soul and make me entirely like Himself.

At other times, when I apply myself to prayer, I feel all my spirit and all my soul lift itself up without any care or effort of mine, and it continues as it were suspended and firmly fixed in

God, as in its center and place of rest.

Equipped to Win
Kay Arthur

Put on the whole armour of God.
EPHESIANS 6:11

My daddy used to tell me that the best defense is a good offense! Beloved, God never intended for the Christian to constantly live on the defensive. We are to storm the gates of hell and demand that Satan's captives be set free. Ours is the victory; we are the ones who are more than conquerors. . . . God's Word says that the gates of hell cannot prevail, cannot stand, against the church; they must give way!

When you read of the Christian's warfare with the enemy in Ephesians 6, God clearly tells you that you are to put on the full armor of God. As you read this description of the Christian's armor, you soon realize that it only covers the front of the soldier! It allows for full protection as long as you don't turn your back! God never sounds retreat, nor do you ever have to wave the flag of surrender. Why? Because the soldier of Christ has the ultimate of weapons. It is the sword of the Spirit which is the Word of God. Thus, we come to the reason Satan would keep us from God's Word. The Word of God is the Christian's only offensive weapon. It is all he needs—nothing more! With it, the Christian is the victor, more than a conqueror; without it, all he can do is defend himself.

PERSEVERING PRAYER

Charles H. Spurgeon

And he went a little farther, and fell on his face, and prayed.
MATTHEW 26:39

*T*here are several instructive features in our Savior's prayer in His hour of trial. It was lonely prayer. He withdrew even from His three favored disciples. Believer, be much in solitary prayer, especially in times of trial.

It was humble prayer. Luke says He knelt, but another evangelist says He "fell on His face." Humility gives us good foothold in prayer. There is no hope of prevalence with God unless we abase ourselves that He may exalt us in due time.

It was filial prayer. "Abba, Father." You will find it a stronghold in the day of trial to plead your adoption. You have no rights as a subject, you have forfeited them by your treason; but nothing can forfeit a child's right to a father's protection. Be not afraid to say, "My Father, hear my cry."

Observe that it was persevering prayer. He prayed three times. Cease not until you prevail. Continue in prayer, and watch in the same with thanksgiving.

Lastly, it was the prayer of resignation. "Nevertheless, not as I will, but as Thou wilt." Yield, and God yields. Let it be as God wills, and God will determine for the best. Be thou content to leave thy prayer in His hands, who knows when to give and how to give and what to give, and what to withhold.

Praying Is a Form of Work

Mrs. Charles E. Cowman

Men ought always to pray, and not to faint.

LUKE 18:1

*T*hat little "ought" is emphatic. It implies obligation as high as heaven. Jesus said, "Men ought always to pray," and added, "and not to faint."

I confess I do not always feel like praying—when, judging by my feelings, there is no one listening to my prayer. And then these words have stirred me to pray:

> *I ought to pray—*
> *I ought always to pray—*
> *I should not grow faint in praying.*

"Praying is a form of work. The farmer ploughs his field often when he does not feel like it, but he confidently expects a crop for his labors.

Once when I knelt for morning prayers I felt a sort of deadness in my soul, and just then the "accuser of the brethren" became busy reminding me of things that had long since been under the Blood. I cried to God for help, and the blessed Comforter reminded me that my Great High Priest was pleading my case, that I must come boldly to the throne of grace. I did, and the enemy was routed! Had I fainted instead of fighting, I could not have received wages because I had not labored fervently in prayer; I could not have reaped because I had not sown."

SAMUEL LOGAN BRENGLE

FATHER PROVIDES

Andrew Murray

"But seek first his kingdom and his righteousness,
and all these things will be given to you as well."

MATTHEW 6:33 NIV

$\mathcal{G}$ive us this day our daily bread." When first the child
has yielded himself to the Father in the care of His
Name, His kingdom, and His Will, he has full liberty
to ask for his daily bread. A master cares for the food of
his servant, a general of his soldiers, a father of his child.
And will not the Father in heaven care for the child
who has in prayer given himself up to His interests?
We may indeed in full confidence say, "Father, I live
for Thy honor and Thy work; I know Thou carest for
me." Consecration to God and His will gives wonderful
liberty in prayer for temporal things: the whole earthly
life is given to the Father's loving care.

The Lord Hears My Voice

Samuel Bagster

Do not be anxious about anything,
but in every situation, by prayer and petition,
with thanksgiving, present your requests to God.

PHILIPPIANS 4:6 NIV

"I love the LORD, because he hath heard my voice and my supplications. Because he hath inclined his ear unto me, therefore will I call upon him as long as I live" (Psalm 116:1–2).

"When ye pray, use not vain repetitions, as the heathen do: for they think that they shall be heard for their much speaking. The Spirit. . .helpeth our infirmities: for we know not what we should pray for as we ought: but the Spirit itself maketh intercession for us with groanings which cannot be uttered" (Matthew 6:7, Romans 8:26).

"I will therefore that men pray every where, lifting up holy hands, without wrath and doubting. Praying always with all prayer and supplication in the Spirit, and watching thereunto with all perseverance and supplication for all saints" (1 Timothy 2:8, Ephesians 6:18).

"If two of you shall agree on earth as touching any thing that they shall ask, it shall be done for them of my Father which is in heaven" (Matthew 18:19).

Our Prayer-Union

Andrew Murray

I am the vine, ye are the branches: He that abideth in me,
and I in him, the same bringeth forth much fruit:
for without me ye can do nothing.

JOHN 15:5

The union between the Vine and the branch is in
very deed a prayer-union. The highest conformity
to Christ, the most blessed participation in the glory
of His heavenly life, is that we take part in His work
of intercession: He and we live ever to pray. In the
experience of our union with Him, praying without
ceasing becomes a possibility, a reality, the holiest and
most blessed part of our holy and blessed fellowship with
God. We have our abode within the veil, in the presence
of the Father. What the Father says, we do; what the
Son says, the Father does. Praying without ceasing is the
earthly manifestation of heaven come down to us, the
foretaste of the life where they rest not day or night in
the song of worship and adoration.

TROUBLE OR TRIUMPH

Kay Arthur

Call upon me in the day of trouble:
I will deliver thee, and thou shalt glorify me.

PSALM 50:15

*W*hen you are in trouble or in need, where do you run for help? What is your first instinct? Do you run to man or to God? When you are hurting or confused, when you don't know what to do, whose counsel do you seek first? Isn't it usually the counsel of another human being rather than the counsel found in waiting upon God in prayer? Why is it? Why do we run to man before we run to God?

What is the problem? Why do so many Christians run to the arm of flesh rather than the arms of our all-sufficient God? I think, beloved, it is because most of us do not really know our God. Why is it that many collapse in the day of trouble and testing? Why is it that Christians are immobilized rather than taking an aggressive stand in the face of fear? It is because Christians, for the most part, cannot boast in the name of their God.

What do I mean when I say "boast in the name of our God"? To boast means to have confidence in, to trust in His name. Therefore, to boast in God's name means to have confidence in His name. In biblical times, a name represented a person's character. God's name represents His character, His attributes, His nature. To know His name is to know Him. To boast in His name is to have confidence in who He is!

LORD OF THE HARVEST

Andrew Murray

"The harvest is plentiful, but the workers are few. Ask the Lord of the harvest, therefore, to send out workers into his harvest field."
LUKE 10:2 NIV

O let us pray for a life so one with Christ that His compassion may stream into us and His Spirit be able to assure us that our prayer avails.

Such a prayer will ask and obtain a twofold blessing. There will first be the desire for the increase of men entirely given up to the service of God. It is a terrible blot upon the Church of Christ that there are times when actual men cannot be found for the service of the Master as ministers, missionaries, or teachers of God's Word. As God's children make this a matter of supplication for their own circle or Church, it will be given. The Lord Jesus is now Lord of the harvest. He has been exalted to bestow gifts—the gifts of the Spirit. His chief gifts are men filled with the Spirit. But the supply and distribution of the gifts depend on the cooperation of Head and members. It is just prayer that will lead to such cooperation; the believing suppliants will be stirred to find the men and the means for the work.

Power in Unity

Andrew Murray

Whatsoever ye shall bind on earth shall be bound in heaven. . . .
For where two or three are gathered together in my name. . .

MATTHEW 18:18, 20

Blessed Lord! It is when we are one in love and desire
that our faith has Thy presence and the Father's answer.
O let the thought of Thy presence and the Father's favor
draw us all nearer to each other.

Grant especially, Blessed Lord, that Thy Church
may believe that it is by the power of united prayer that
she can bind and loose in heaven, that Satan can be
cast out, that souls can be saved, that mountains can be
removed, that the kingdom can be hastened. And grant,
good Lord! that in the circle with which I pray, the
prayer of the Church may indeed be the power through
which Thy Name and Word are glorified. Amen.

AT HIS TABLE

Brother Lawrence

You prepare a table before me in the presence of my enemies.
You anoint my head with oil; my cup overflows.
PSALM 23:5 NIV

I think it proper to inform you after what manner I consider myself before God, whom I behold as my King. I consider myself as the most wretched of men, full of sores and corruption, and who has committed all sorts of crimes against his King. Touched with a sensible regret, I confess to Him all my wickedness; I ask His forgiveness; I abandon myself in His hands that He may do what He pleases with me. The King, full of mercy and goodness, very far from chastising me, embraces me with love, makes me eat at His table, serves me with His own hands, gives me the key to His treasures; He converses and delights Himself with me incessantly, in a thousand ways, and treats me in all respects as His favorite. It is thus I consider myself from time to time in His holy presence.

THE FATHER'S INTEREST
Andrew Murray

Our Father which art in heaven, Hallowed be thy name.
Thy kingdom come. Thy will be done. . . .
LUKE 11:2

There are two sorts of prayer: personal and intercessory.
The latter ordinarily occupies the lesser part of our time
and energy. This may not be. Christ has opened the
school of prayer specially to train intercessors for the
great work of bringing down, by their faith and prayer,
the blessings of His work and love on the world around.
There can be no deep growth in prayer unless this be
made our aim. The little child may ask of the father
only what it needs for itself; and yet it soon learns to say,
"Give some for sister, too." But the grown-up son, who
only lives for the father's interest and takes charge of
the father's business, asks more largely and gets all that
is asked. And Jesus would train us to the blessed life of
consecration and service, in which our interests are all
subordinate to the name and the kingdom and the will of
the Father.

Receive Ye!

Andrew Murray

And with that he breathed on them and said,
"Receive the Holy Spirit."
JOHN 20:22 NIV

*F*ather in heaven! Thou didst send Thy Son to reveal Thyself to us, Thy Father-love, and all that that love has for us. And He has taught us that the gift above all gifts which Thou wouldest bestow in answer to prayer is the Holy Spirit.

O my Father! I come to Thee with this prayer; there is nothing I would—may I not say, I do—desire so much as to be filled with the Spirit, the Holy Spirit. The blessings He brings are so unspeakable and just what I need. He sheds abroad Thy love in the heart and fills it with Thyself. I long for this. He breathes the mind and life of Christ in me, so that I live as He did, in and for the Father's love. I long for this. He endues with power from on high for all my walk and work. I long for this. O Father! I beseech Thee, give me this day the fullness of Thy Spirit.

Father! I ask this, resting on the words of my Lord: *"How much more the Holy Spirit."* I do believe that Thou hearest my prayer; I receive now what I ask; Father! I claim and I take it: the fullness of Thy Spirit as mine.

HOW MUCH MORE?

Andrew Murray

*Or what man is there of you, whom if his son ask bread,
will he give him a stone? Or if he ask a fish, will he give him a
serpent? . . . How much more shall your Father which is in
heaven give good things to them that ask him?*

MATTHEW 7:9–11

$\mathcal{O}$ur Lord proceeds further to confirm what He had
said of the certainty of an answer to prayer. To remove
all doubt and show us on that sure ground His promise
rests, He appeals to what everyone has seen and
experienced here on earth. We are all children and know
what we expected of our fathers. We are fathers, or
continually see them, and everywhere we look upon it as
the most natural thing there can be, for a father to hear
his child. And the Lord asks us to look up from earthly
parents, of whom the best are but evil, and to calculate
how much more the heavenly Father will give good gifts to
them that ask Him. Jesus would lead us up to see that as
much greater as God is than sinful man, so much greater
our assurance ought to be that He will more surely than
any earthly father grant our childlike petitions. As much
greater as God is than man, so much surer is it that
prayer will be heard with the Father in heaven than with
a father on earth.

LOST AND FOUND

Charles H. Spurgeon

I looked for him but did not find him.
SONG OF SONGS 3:1 NIV

*T*ell me where you lost the company of Christ, and I will tell you the most likely place to find Him. Have you lost Christ in the closet by restraining prayer? Then it is there you must seek and find Him. Did you lose Christ by sin? You will find Christ in no other way but by the giving up of the sin, and seeking by the Holy Spirit to mortify the member in which the lust doth dwell. Do you lose Christ by neglecting the Scriptures? You must find Christ in the Scriptures. It is a true proverb, "Look for a thing where you dropped it, it is there." So look for Christ where you lost Him, for He has not gone away.

One would have thought you would never have parted with such a precious Friend, whose presence is so sweet, whose words are so comforting, and whose company is so dear to you! How is it that you did not watch Him every moment for fear of losing sight of Him? Go on seeking, for it is dangerous to be without thy Lord. With thine whole heart seek Him, and He will be found of thee; only give thyself thoroughly up to the search, and verily, thou shalt yet discover Him to thy joy and gladness.

CHRIST, MY LAW

Andrew Murray

Let this mind be in you,
which was also in Christ Jesus.

PHILIPPIANS 2:5

*L*et us yield our hearts to God in prayer, for Him to search us and discover in us whether the life of Christ has actually been the law that we have taken for the guide of our life. I do not speak about attainment, but let us ask, Have I actually said: "Oh, how blessed it would be! Oh, this is what I covet, and what I wait upon God for! I want to live for God in the way Christ lived"? It almost sounds as if it were too high and presumptuous. But what does Christ mean when He said so often: "As I, even so you; as I loved, even so love one another; as I kept the commandments of My Father, so, if ye keep His commandments, ye shall abide in My love"? What does the Holy Spirit mean when He says, "Let this mind be in you which was also in Christ Jesus, who made Himself of no reputation, but humbled Himself and became obedient unto death"? The mind of Christ must be my mind, my disposition, and my life.

Joy in Our Daily Walk

❧

I am crucified with Christ: nevertheless I live; yet not I,
but Christ liveth in me: and the life which I now live
in the flesh I live by the faith of the Son of God,
who loved me, and gave himself for me.

GALATIANS 2:20

The Paralysis of Analysis

Brother Andrew

Whatever you have learned or received or heard from me, or seen in me—put it into practice. And the God of peace will be with you.

PHILIPPIANS 4:9 NIV

As we spend time in scripture and in prayer, it's important not to get sidetracked in trying to determine whether we've received an official call from God or whether we have a clear indication that we are doing God's will. It's too easy to get so caught up in the paralysis of analysis that we fail to act. Most of us often have the idea that God must have a special calling in our lives. If we have no such calling from God, then we have not been selected by Him for special service, and we can only live out our lives as drones in the kingdom, one monotonous and unimportant day at a time. . . . That is our idea, not God's.

We must never make our dreams for success or accomplishment as God's purpose for us. God's end, His purpose for us, is the process.

God has given us in scripture a full revelation of His nature and His character. And He has given us an unmistakably clear mandate to share Him and His Word with those who have not heard. If we focus on obeying Him on a daily basis—wherever we are—He will lead us where He wants us to go and to the people He wants us to reach.

OBEDIENCE

from *Daily Strength for Daily Needs*

Obey my voice, and I will be your God, and ye shall be my people:
and walk ye in all the ways that I have commanded you,
that it may be well unto you.

JEREMIAH 7:23

And oft, when in my heart was heard Thy timely mandate,
I deferred the task in smoother walks to stray;
But thee I now would serve more strictly, if I may.
W. WORDSWORTH

*P*ray to Him to give you what scripture calls "an honest and good heart," or "a perfect heart" and, without waiting, begin at once to obey Him with the best heart you have. Any obedience is better than none. You have to seek His face; obedience is the only way of seeing Him. All your duties are obediences. To do what He bids is to obey Him, and to obey Him is to approach Him. Every act of obedience is an approach—an approach to Him who is not far off, though He seems so, but close behind this visible screen of things which hides Him from us.

J. H. NEWMAN

*A*s soon as we lay ourselves entirely at His feet, we have enough light given us to guide our own steps; as the foot soldier, who hears nothing of the councils that determine the course of the great battle he is in, hears plainly enough the word of command which he must himself obey.

GEORGE ELIOT

GRUDGES

John Henry Jowett

"Do not seek revenge or bear a grudge against anyone among your people, but love your neighbor as yourself. I am the LORD."

LEVITICUS 19:18 NIV

*H*ow searching is that demand upon the soul! My forgiveness of my brother is to be complete. No sullenness is to remain, no sulky temper which so easily gives birth to thunder and lightning. There is to be no painful aloofness, no assumption of a superiority which rains contempt upon the offender. When I forgive, I am not to carry any powder forward on the journey. I am to empty out all my explosives, all my ammunition of anger and revenge. I am not to "bear any grudge."

I cannot meet this demand. It is altogether beyond me. I might utter words of forgiveness, but I cannot reveal a clear, bright, blue sky without a touch of storm brewing anywhere. But the Lord of grace can do it for me. He can change my weather. He can create a new climate. He can "renew a right spirit within me," and in that holy atmosphere nothing shall live which seeks to poison and destroy. Grudges shall die "like cloud-spots in the dawn." Revenge, that was full creation of the unclean, feverish soul, shall give place to goodwill, the strong genial presence which makes its home in a new heart.

THE CALLING

Brother Andrew

Then saith he unto his disciples, The harvest truly is plenteous,
but the labourers are few; Pray ye therefore the Lord of the harvest,
that he will send forth labourers into his harvest.

MATTHEW 9:37–38

*T*he real calling of God is not to a certain place or career but to everyday obedience. Then, as we follow His everyday call, He opens doors to where He wants us to go and closes doors to where He does not want us to go. That way, faithfulness to God's calling is within our reach every day.

On the other hand, if we agonize over whether we have received a special call, we waste valuable time and energy and, in effect, limit the work of God in our lives.

How do we prepare to respond to that call? Part of the preparation is God's doing, and part of it must be ours. God's preparation of us began long before we decided to accept His call. The fact is, God has been using all of the events and experiences of our lives to prepare us for the kind of service He's calling us to now. Whether our past was happy or sad, godly or sordid, God is building on that experience to make us into effective servants for Him.

IMPOSSIBLE PROOFS

Andrew Murray

For with God nothing shall be impossible.

LUKE 1:37

*Y*our religious life is every day to be a proof that God works impossibilities; your religious life is to be a series of impossibilities made possible and actual by God's almighty power. That is what the Christian needs. He has an almighty God that he worships, and he must learn to understand: I do not want a little of God's power, but I want—with reverence be it said—the whole of God's omnipotence to keep me right and to live like a Christian.

No Limits

Ken Abraham

*He said unto them, Have ye received
the Holy Ghost since ye believed?*

ACTS 19:2

Surrender completely every area of your life to the Lordship of Christ. Hold nothing back. Give Him all the keys. There's no time for hypocrisy now. You cannot attempt to bargain with God ("I'll give you this area, God, if You will give me that gift") if you hope to enter into holiness. As you obey Christ and allow Him to have absolute control in your life, He will fill you with His Spirit. He will then continue to expand your capacity to be filled for the rest of your life, producing more and more of His character—the fruit of the Spirit—in you.

This is a never-ending process. You can never plumb the depths of God's love. You will never exhaust His fresh supply of resources in your life. There is no height, nor depth, no limit at all to how deeply you can grow in Christ. His Spirit will continue to extend your horizons.

Maybe that explains why truly holy people rarely become bored. Just about the time you say, "Okay, God, I think I've got a handle on this Christian life; I think I've gone as far as I can go," He says, "Oh, really? Well, open wide, because I am going to do something more in your heart, something your mind has not even yet conceived!" What an exciting way to live!

Revisiting Old Altars

John Henry Jowett

"I will build an altar to God,
who answered me in the day of my distress."

GENESIS 35:3 NIV

It is a blessed thing to revisit our early altars. It is good to return to the haunts of early vision. Places and things have their sanctifying influences and can recall us to lost experiences. I know a man to whom the scent of a white, wild rose is always a call to prayer. I know another to whom Grasmere is always the window of holy vision. Sometimes a particular pew in a particular church can throw the heavens open, and we see the Son of God. The old Sunday school has sometimes taken an old man back to his childhood and back to his God. So I do not wonder that God led Jacob back to Bethel, and that in the old place of blessing he re-consecrated himself to the Lord.

It is a revelation of the loving-kindness of God that we have all these helps to the recovery of past experiences. Let us use them with reverence. And in our early days let us make them. Let us build altars of communion which in later life we shall love to revisit. Let us make our early home "the house of God and the gate of heaven." Let us multiply deeds of service which will make countless places fragrant for all our after-years.

THE BEAUTY OF THE DEEP

F. B. Meyer

Deep calls to deep.

PSALM 42:7 NIV

*W*e need to dwell deep, to have a life beneath a life, to have windows in our heart that look across the river into the unseen and eternal. The pictures that fascinate are those that suggest more than they reveal, in which the blue distance fades into the heavens, and the light mist veils mountain, moorland, and sea. Oh for the peace that passeth understanding, the joy that is unspeakable and full of glory, the deep things which eye hath not seen, nor ear heard, nor the heart of man conceived!

RIGHTEOUS ANGER,
UNRIGHTEOUS ANGER

Charles H. Spurgeon

"Is it right for you to be angry. . .?"
JONAH 4:9 NIV

*A*nger is not always or necessarily sinful, but it has such a tendency to run wild that whenever it displays itself, we should be quick to question its character with this inquiry, "Doest thou well to be angry?" It may be that we can answer "Yes." We do well when we are angry with sin because of the wrong which it commits against our good and gracious God, or with ourselves because we remain so foolish after so much divine instruction, or with others when the sole cause of anger is the evil which they do. He who is not angry at transgression becomes a partaker in it. Sin is a loathsome and hateful thing, and no renewed heart can patiently endure it. God Himself is angry with the wicked every day, and it is written in His Word, "Ye that love the Lord, hate evil."

Far more frequently it is to be feared that our anger is not commendable or even justifiable, and then we must answer, "No." If we cannot control our tempers, what has grace done for us? We must not make natural infirmity an excuse for sin, but we must fly to the cross and pray to the Lord to crucify our tempers and renew us in gentleness and meekness after His own image.

PLACE OF PRIVILEGE

Hannah Whitall Smith

The LORD is my rock, and my fortress, and my deliverer;
my God, my strength, in whom I will trust; my buckler,
and the horn of my salvation, and my high tower.

PSALM 18:2

*B*etter and sweeter than health or friends or money
or fame or ease or prosperity is the adorable will of
our God. It gilds the darkest hours with a divine halo
and sheds brightest sunshine on the gloomiest paths.
He always reigns who has made it His kingdom, and
nothing can go amiss to Him. Surely then, it is only a
glorious privilege that is opening before you when I tell
you that the first step you must take in order to enter
into the life hid with Christ in God is that of entire
consecration. I beg of you not to look at it as a hard
and stern demand. You must do it gladly, thankfully,
enthusiastically. You must go in on what I call the
privilege side of consecration; and I can assure you, from
the universal testimony of all who have tried it, that you
will find it the happiest place you have ever entered yet.

Give and It Shall Be Given

Charles H. Spurgeon

Whoever refreshes others will be refreshed.
Proverbs 11:25 NIV

We are here taught the great lesson that to get we must give, that to accumulate we must scatter, that to make ourselves happy we must make others happy, and that in order to become spiritually vigorous we must seek the spiritual good of others. In watering others, we are ourselves watered. How? Our efforts to be useful bring out our powers for usefulness. We have latent talents and dormant faculties, which are brought to light by exercise. Our strength for labor is hidden even from ourselves until we venture forth to fight the Lord's battles or to climb the mountains of difficulty. We do not know what tender sympathies we possess until we try to dry the widow's tears and soothe the orphan's grief. We often find in attempting to teach others that we gain instruction for ourselves. Oh, what gracious lessons some of us have learned at sick beds! We went to teach the scriptures; we came away blushing that we knew so little of them. In our converse with poor saints, we are taught the way of God more perfectly for ourselves and get a deeper insight into divine truth. So that watering others makes us humble. We discover how much grace there is where we had not looked for it, and how much the poor saint may outstrip us in knowledge.

Total Forgiveness

R. T. Kendall

And we know that all things work together for good to them that love God, to them who are the called according to his purpose.

ROMANS 8:28

What is God saying to you? Forgive yourself. He's trying to show you right now how you can do it. Our gracious God comes from behind to shape your past so that, if you will believe Him and give Him time, you will come to see that His hand was with you even at your worst moment. Total forgiveness shows God's sovereign plan in everything. If you really do forgive someone, show that you mean it by bringing in God's total sovereignty.

Think of all that you have done that is wrong. All that is bad. All that is wicked. Can anything be better than this—that all things "work together" for good?

Oh, the relief I feel—to think that God was with me in my worst moment! But this is the sovereign grace of God. Only a God like that can do it. He can shape your past and take your worst moment and, in time, so redeem your past that you can look back and not wish to change anything. This is the God of the Bible.

UNION WITH CHRIST

Andrew Murray

Behold, now is the day of salvation.

2 CORINTHIANS 6:2

Let any Christian begin, then, and he will speedily experience how the blessing of the present moment is passed on to the next. It is the unchanging Jesus to whom he links himself; it is the power of a divine life, in its unbroken continuity, that takes possession of him. The *do it now* of the present moment—a little thing though it seems—is nothing less than the beginning of the ever-present now, which is the mystery and the glory of eternity. Therefore, Christian, abide in Christ. Do it now.

DIVERSITY, NOT UNIFORMITY

Dr. F. F. Bruce

Now there are diversities of gifts, but the same Spirit.
And there are differences of administrations,
but the same Lord. And there are diversities of operations,
but it is the same God which worketh all in all.

1 CORINTHIANS 12:4–6

*D*iversity, not uniformity, is the mark of God's handiwork. It is so in nature; it is so in grace, too, and nowhere more so than in the Christian community. Here are many men and women with the most diverse kinds of parentage, environment, temperament, and capacity. Not only so, but since they became Christians they have been endowed by God with a great variety of spiritual gifts as well. Yet because and by means of that diversity, all can cooperate for the good of the whole. Whatever kind of service is to be rendered in the church, let it be rendered heartily and faithfully by those divinely qualified, whether it be prophesying, teaching, admonishing, administering, making material gifts, sick-visiting, or performing any other kind of ministry.

To illustrate what he means, Paul uses the figure of a human body in 1 Corinthians 12:12–27. Each part of the body has its own distinctive work to do, yet in a healthy body all the parts function harmoniously and interdependently for the good of the whole body. So should it be in the church, which is the body of Christ.

Take My Life and Let It Be

Ken Abraham

The blood of Jesus. . .purifies us from all sin.
1 John 1:7 niv

A musician whose words are worth reviewing was the remarkable nineteenth-century songwriter Frances Ridley Havergal. Some of her classic hymns include "Take My Life and Let it Be" and "Like a River Glorious." Miss Havergal often acknowledged that the keys to her success were surrender and cleansing. On surrender she said, "I saw it as a flash of electric light, and what you see you can never un-see. There must be full surrender before there can be full blessedness. God admits you by one into the other. . . . So I just yielded myself to Him and utterly trusted Him to keep me."

Later she wrote of her own experience, "The wonderful and glorious blessing, which so many Christians are testifying to have found, was suddenly, marvelously, sent to me last winter; and life is now what I never imagined life on earth could be. . . ." Furthermore, Frances Havergal saw clearly that the cleansing blood of Jesus did a complete, purifying work in her heart. Basing her convictions upon the scripture verse "the blood of Jesus. . .cleanseth us from all sin" (1 John 1:7), Miss Havergal became convinced that not only did the blood of Jesus cleanse past sins, but believers could depend upon Christ's blood for continual cleansing.

The Big Difference

R. T. Kendall

God was with him.
Acts 7:9

*T*here was something at work in Joseph's life that was wonderful and positive, a gift that God gave him. One of the keys to understanding Joseph is provided by Stephen in Acts 7:9—"God was with him." If God is with us, there is no impediment, no personality difficulty, no problem about class background that can stand in the way of him making us a mighty instrument for our day. God was with Joseph and he had a gift, a gift that would shape his own life and also the life of Israel. God gave him dreams. Now that may not sound very impressive. Whoever would have thought that a gift like that could mean so much? And God has given to you something that nobody else can do. Because God made you different.

It is sometimes said of a particular person, "When God made so-and-so, he threw the mold away." But wait. He threw the mold away when he made us! We are all different from anybody else. To affirm the gift that God has given us is a way of glorifying our Creator. Subsequent events in Joseph's life would reveal that this gift, this dreaming which apparently included an ability to interpret dreams, saved his own life and the lives of his family.

THE MOST DELICATE MISSION ON EARTH

Oswald Chambers

❦

. . .the friend of the bridegroom. . .
JOHN 3:29

*G*oodness and purity ought never to attract attention to themselves, they ought simply to be magnets to draw to Jesus Christ. If my holiness is not drawing towards Him, it is not holiness of the right order but an influence that will awaken inordinate affection and lead souls away into side-eddies. A beautiful saint may be a hindrance if he does not present Jesus Christ but only what Christ has done for him. He will leave the impression—"What a fine character that man is!" That is not being a true friend of the Bridegroom; I am increasing all the time, He is not. In order to maintain this friendship and loyalty to the Bridegroom, we have to be more careful of our moral and vital relationship to Him than of any other thing, even of obedience.

Sometimes there is nothing to obey, the only thing to do is to maintain a vital connection with Jesus Christ, to see that nothing interferes with that. Only occasionally do we have to obey.

When a crisis arises we have to find out what God's will is, but the greater part of the life is not conscious obedience but the maintenance of this relationship—the friend of the Bridegroom.

Personal Holiness
J. I. Packer

And to put on the new self, created to be like
God in true righteousness and holiness.

EPHESIANS 4:24 NIV

Christians are called to oppose the world. But how,
in this case, can that be done? Credible opposition to
secular ideologies can be shown by speaking and writing,
but credible opposition to unholiness can only be shown
by holy living (see Ephesians 5:3–14). Ecumenical goals
for the church are defined nowadays in terms of the
quest for social, racial, and economic justice, but it would
be far healthier if our first aim was agreed to be personal
and relational holiness in every believer's life. Much as
the modern West needs the impact of Christian truth, it
needs the impact of Christian holiness even more, both
to demonstrate that godliness is the true humanness
and to keep community life from rotting to destruction.
The pursuit of holiness is thus no mere private hobby,
nor merely a path for a select few, but a vital element in
Christian mission strategy today. The world's greatest
need is the personal holiness of Christian people.

THE THREE GARDENS

John Henry Jowett

"In the midst of the street of it, and on either side of the river,
was there the tree of life, which bare twelve manner of fruits,
and yielded her fruit every month: and the leaves of
the tree were for the healing of the nations."

REVELATION 22:2

The Bible opens with a garden. It closes with a garden. The first is the Paradise that was lost. The last is Paradise regained. And between the two there is a third garden, the garden of Gethsemane. And it is through the unspeakable bitterness and desolation of Gethsemane that we find again the glorious garden through which flows "the river of life." Without Gethsemane, no New Jerusalem! Without its mysterious and unfathomable night, no blessed sunrise of eternal hope! "We were reconciled to God by the death of His Son." (Romans 5:10)

Privileges easily come to be esteemed as rights. And even grace itself can lose the strength of heavenly favor and can be received and used as our due. "Gethsemane can I forget?" Yes I can, and in the forgetfulness I lose the sacred awe of my redemption, and I miss the real glory of "Paradise regained."

"Ye are not your own; ye are bought with a price." (1 Corinthians 6:19–20) That is the remembrance that keeps the spirit lowly and that fills the heart with love for Him "whose I am" and whom I ought to serve.

Joy in Praise and Worship

%

Enter into his gates with thanksgiving,
and into his courts with praise:
be thankful unto him, and bless his name.

PSALM 100:4

Other Gods

John Henry Jowett

Thou shalt have no other gods before me.
EXODUS 20:3

If we kept that commandment, all the other commandments would be obeyed. If we secure this queen bee, we are given the swarm. To put nothing "before" God! What is left in the circle of obedience? God first, always and everywhere. Nothing allowed to usurp His throne for an hour! I was once allowed to sit on an earthly throne for a few seconds, but even that is not to be allowed with the throne of God. Nothing is to share His sovereignty, even for a moment. His dominion is to be unconditional and unbroken. "Thou shalt have no other gods beside Me."

But we have many gods we set upon His throne. We put money there, and fame and pleasure and ease. Yes, we sometimes usurp God's throne, and we ourselves dare to sit there for days and weeks and years at a time. Self is the idol, and we enthrone it, and we fall down and worship it. But no peace comes from such sovereignty, and no deep and vital joy. For the real King is not dead, He is out and about, and our poor little monarchy is as the reign of the midge on a summer's night. Our real kingship is in the acknowledgment of the King of kings. When we worship Him, and Him only, He will ask us to sit on His throne.

CHIMES OF PRAISE
William A. Quale

Let everything that has breath praise the LORD.
Praise the LORD.

PSALM 150:6 NIV

O what a heyday of music the insects make in August!
I revel in it. The crickets chirp. The tree toad sets his
instrument going. The wild bees hum drowsily enough
to put you to sleep. The tame bees go into the clover
blossoms and drink them dry at a single gulp. Then a
score of voices chime coming from what insects I cannot
tell but full of all that blessed gladness which God has
so kindly put into the heart of every living thing. I
listen and praise. Such a happy world, so full of song.
In August birds have grown tired singing or are grown
too fat to sing, and in any case sing but little. Then the
insects tune up. At night, the tree toads set up a storm of
minstrels.

At noon and night and the day through, you shall
hear the strident locust which in the spring you seldom
hear, save at evening. How the locust's voice—with its
blur of sound—delights my ear. I go and stand near a
branch or a hedge to wait till he tunes up again and fairly
stumbles in his tune so full of life. So is the August heat
squeezing this music out of him as honey from the comb.

Singing for Holiness

Donald Grey Barnhouse

What time I am afraid, I will trust in thee. In God I will
praise his word, in God I have put my trust; I will not fear. . . .

PSALM 56:3–4

*R*obert Murray M'Cheyne, the great Scottish
preacher, was a very gifted man in many ways. He had
no inconsiderable knowledge of music, and his voice
was frequently heard in praise to God. In his diary,
which is one of the outstanding documents of its kind
in Christian literature, we see the growth of this great
soul as he so earnestly sought after God's own holiness.
He wrote, "Is it the desire of my heart to be made
altogether holy? Is there any sin I wish to retain? Is sin a
grief to me, the sudden risings and overcoming thereof
especially? Lord, Thou knowest all things. Thou knowest
that I hate all sin and desire to be made altogether like
Thee. . . . Felt much deadness and much grief that I
cannot grieve for this deadness. Towards evening revived.
Got a calm spirit through Psalmody and prayer."

If you are despondent or discouraged, speak now to
the Lord who dwells within your heart. Say to Him that
you know you have been redeemed, and acknowledge
His presence and His character as being more than
worthy of praise. Ask Him to kindle the song. Have it on
your lips even if you do not feel it in your heart.

Sing Unto the Lord a New Song

Samuel Bagster

He put a new song in my mouth, a hymn of praise to our God.
Many will see and fear the LORD and put their trust in him.

PSALM 40:3 NIV

Sing aloud unto God our strength: make a joyful noise unto the God of Jacob. Take a psalm, and bring hither the timbrel, the pleasant harp with the psaltery" (Psalm 81:1–2 KJV). "He hath put a new song in my mouth, even praise unto our God: many shall see it, and fear, and shall trust in the LORD" (Psalm 40:3).

"Be strong and of a good courage; be not afraid, neither be thou dismayed: for the LORD thy God is with thee whithersoever thou goest" (Joshua 1:9). "The joy of the LORD is your strength" (Nehemiah 8:10). "Paul. . . thanked God, and took courage" (Acts 28:15).

"Knowing the time, that now it is high time to awake out of sleep: for now is our salvation nearer than when we believed" (Romans 13:11).

"The night is far spent, the day is at hand: let us therefore cast off the works of darkness, and let us put on the armour of light. Let us walk honestly, as in the day; not in rioting and drunkenness, not in chambering and wantonness, not in strife and envying. But put ye on the Lord Jesus Christ, and make not provision for the flesh, to fulfil the lusts thereof" (Romans 13:12–14).

I Praise Thee, O God

Susanna Wesley/Edith Dean

He taught me also, and said unto me, Let thine heart
retain my words: keep my commandments, and live.
Get wisdom, get understanding: forget it not;
neither decline from the words of my mouth.

PROVERBS 4:4–5

I praise Thee, O God, for illuminating my mind and
for enabling me to prove demonstratively that Thy
wisdom is as infinite as Thy power. Help me to use these
discoveries to praise and love and obey Thee, and may I
be exceedingly careful that my affections keep pace with
my knowledge.

May I adore the mystery I cannot comprehend.
Help me to be not too curious in prying into those secret
things that are known only to Thee, O God, nor too
rash in censuring what I do not understand. May I not
perplex myself about those methods of providence that
seem to me involved and intricate, but resolve them into
Thine infinite wisdom, who knowest the spirits of all
flesh and dost best understand how to govern those souls
Thou hast created.

We are of yesterday and know nothing. But Thy
boundless mind comprehends, at one view, all things,
past, present, and future; and as Thou dost see all things,
Thou dost best understand what is good and proper for
each individual and for me, with relation to both worlds.
So deal with me, O my God. Amen.

MUSIC IS A UNIVERSAL LANGUAGE

Dan Dick

Begin the music, strike the timbrel,
play the melodious harp and lyre.

PSALM 81:2 NIV

*B*eth was different when she was singing. Somehow the pressures of the world disappeared when the music filled her head and heart. Her whole life felt somehow lighter, brighter, when she lifted her voice in praise through song. Music was the best expression of who she was and what she believed. Music made God real to Beth.

Music is a universal language. Every culture has its music, and it is revered as one of the finest arts. Music brings people together and can move us closer to God. God loves music and the spirit from which music springs. The quality is not nearly as important as the intention of the heart. Sing out to God, and He will bless you richly.

Music touches my heart in a special way, Lord.
Speak to me through the beauty of music.
Touch me day by day. Amen.

Southern Exposure

Donald Grey Barnhouse

*And at midnight Paul and Silas prayed, and sang praises
unto God: and the prisoners heard them. And suddenly there
was a great earthquake, so that the foundations of the prison
were shaken: and immediately all the doors were opened,
and every one's bands were loosed.*

Acts 16:25–26

*I*n the book of Ezekiel there is a wonderful prophecy of
the Kingdom age and the glories of that time. There is a
description of the temple of God and its surroundings.
In the midst of the description there is a beautiful
phrase about the apartments of the singers: "Without
the inner gate were the chambers of the singers. . .and
their prospect was toward the south" (Ezekiel 40:44).
Southern exposure! Their life was the life of song, and
their chambers were filled with the sunshine of God.

In prison Paul and Silas "prayed, and sang praises
unto God: and the prisoners heard them" (Acts 16:25).
There was southern exposure at midnight; there was a
jail filled with the sunshine of God's blessings. Their
backs were lacerated with the scourge, and they were
in circumstances that called for weeping, as far as the
world is concerned. They were not even facing toward
the frigid north; they were in the darkness of the world's
midnight. Happy are the men who learn this truth and
bring the sunlight of God into the chambers of their
dwelling, always looking out over the southern prospect
which God has given them.

THE MAN CHRIST JESUS

T. C. Horton and Charles E. Hurlburt

For there is one God, and one mediator between
God and men, the man Christ Jesus.

1 TIMOTHY 2:5

*W*e have considered Christ as Mediator, and now
we have the emphasis upon Christ, our Mediator, as
the Man Christ Jesus. In these days when He is being
demeaned by so many who are robbing Him of His
Deity, we should rejoice in the privilege offered us of
magnifying Him as both man and God. "Great is the
mystery of Godliness—God manifest in the flesh."
No picture in the Bible is so marvelously thrilling, so
calculated to convince and convert, as that of God dying
for men. Hold Him in your thoughts and see Him
today—arms outstretched above a blood-stained body,
saying, "Come unto Me. I will give you rest."

Oh, Thou crucified, risen God-Man, we adore
Thee. Guide us today in our worship and work for Thee.
Amen.

First, My Brother
John Henry Jowett

Therefore if thou bring thy gift to the altar, and there
rememberest that thy brother hath ought against thee;
leave there thy gift before the altar, and go thy way; first be
reconciled to thy brother, and then come and offer thy gift.

MATTHEW 5:23–24

First be reconciled to thy brother." We are to put first things first. When we bring a gift unto the Lord, He looks at the hand that brings it. If the hand is defiled the gift is rejected. "Wash you, make you clean." "First be reconciled to thy brother, and then come and offer thy gift."

All this tells us why some resplendent gifts are rejected and why some commonplace gifts are received amid heavenly song. This is why the widow's mite goes shining through the years. The hand that offered it was hallowed and purified with sacrifice. Shall we say that in that palm there was something akin to the pierced hands of the Lord? The mite had intimate associations with the Cross. And it also tells me why so much of our public worship is offensive to our Lord. We come to the church from a broken friendship. Some holy thing has been broken on the way. Someone's estate has been invaded and his treasure spoiled. Someone has been wronged, and God will not touch our gift. "Leave there thy gift; first be reconciled to thy brother."

GUIDE OTHERS TO GLORY

Susanna Wesley/Edith Dean

Giving no offence in any thing. . .but in all things approving
ourselves as the ministers of God, in much patience, in afflictions,
in necessities, in distresses. . .by pureness, by knowledge, by long
suffering, by kindness, by the Holy Ghost, by love unfeigned. . . .

2 CORINTHIANS 6:3–4, 6

*T*he training Susanna Wesley gave her children is
indicated by this letter she wrote her eldest son Samuel,
who also became a preacher:

> *Consider well what a separation from the world,*
> *what purity, what devotion, what exemplary*
> *virtue, are required in those who are to guide others*
> *to glory. . . . Begin and end the day with Him*
> *who is the Alpha and Omega, and if you really*
> *experience what it is to love God, you will redeem*
> *all the time you can for His more immediate service.*
> *Endeavor to act upon principle and do not live like*
> *the rest of mankind, who pass through the world*
> *like straws upon a river, which are carried which*
> *way the stream or wind drive them. . . . Whenever*
> *you are tempted to the commission of any sin or*
> *the omission of any duty, pause and say to yourself,*
> *What am I about to do? God sees me.*

Susanna Wesley's story is one of uncommon misery,
hardship, and failure. Spiritually, however, it is a life of
true riches, glory, and victory, for she never lost her high
ideals nor her sublime faith.

Thanksgiving

Donald Grey Barnhouse

*Enter his gates with thanksgiving and his courts
with praise; give thanks to him and praise his name.*

PSALM 100:4 NIV

$\mathcal{A}$ well-known layman was asked to return thanks
before the meal. I have heard the blessing asked
hundreds of times, but suddenly my attention was
aroused. The man who was praying said, "We thank
Thee for all these gifts, for our food, for our water. . . ."
Thank God for the water. . . . I have asked the blessing
before thousands of meals, but that day for the first time,
I thanked the Lord in spirit and in truth for common
ordinary water, and for the Living Water. I then began to
think of other common things for which we never thank
God and began thanking Him. What are you really
thankful for? Do you realize that God tells us we are to
be thankful for everything?

If difficulties reach us personally, we should take
the attitude which the Spirit taught Paul when he
said, "Most gladly therefore will I rather glory in my
infirmities, that the power of Christ may rest upon me"
(2 Corinthians 12:9). Since we know that all things
work together for the good of those who love the Lord
(Romans 8:28), we must take the attitude of thankfulness
for anything that the Lord sends to us.

Is Thanksgiving Always Possible?

Donald Grey Barnhouse

*Let them sacrifice thank offerings and
tell of his works with songs of joy.*

PSALM 107:22 NIV

God's definite will for the believer is that he shall
be a fountain of praise and that his life shall be in
thanksgiving to God at all times and in all circumstances.

The Lord God, who is the Author of all our
blessings, appreciates, desires, and even seeks our praise
and thanksgiving. . . .

We are to thank God in all things; the Lord knows
what is best for us, and He is ordering the course of
our life, bringing the details to pass in the time and
manner of His desire. He has never made a mistake, and
what He allows to come into the life of His child is for
the good of that child and for the glory of God. Any
chastisement that ever reaches us comes for our profit,
that we might be partakers of His holiness (Hebrews
12:10).

It is wonderful that a man who has been through
sufferings akin to those of Job should cry out in
desire for a heart to praise the Lord. Such desire is
proof of confidence and trust in the Father, for it is
the acknowledgement that He does all things well.
Thanksgiving in all things, this is the will of God.

GOD IS A CONSUMING FIRE
George MacDonald

For our God is a consuming fire.
HEBREWS 12:29

*A*ll that is not beautiful in the beloved, all that comes between and is not of love's kind, must be destroyed. God is a consuming fire. If this be hard to understand, it is as the simple, absolute truth is hard to understand. It may be centuries of ages before a man comes to see a truth—ages of strife, of effort, of aspiration. But when once he does see it, it is so plain that he wonders how he could have lived without seeing it. That he did not understand it sooner was simply and only that he did not see it. To see a truth, to know what it is, to understand it, and to love it, are all one.

He is a consuming fire, that only that which cannot be consumed may stand forth eternal. It is the nature of God, so terribly pure that it destroys all that is not pure as fire, which demands like purity in our worship.

God—
My Strength and Song

John Henry Jowett

The LORD is my strength and song.
PSALM 118:14

*Y*es, first of all "my strength" and then "my song"!
For what song can there be where there is languor and
fainting? What brave music can be born in an organ
which is short of breath? There must first be strength if
we would have fine harmonies. And so the good Lord
comes to the songless, and with holy power He brings
the gift of "saving health."

"And my song"! For when life is healthy, it instinc-
tively breaks into song. The happy, contented soul goes
about the ways of life humming its satisfactions to itself,
and is now and again heard by the passerby. The Lord
fills the life with instinctive music. When life is holy, it
becomes musical with His praise.

So here I see the appointed order in Christian
service. It is futile to try to make people joyful unless we
do it by seeking first to make them strong. First the good
and then the truly happy! First the holy and then the
musical. First God and the breath of His Holy Spirit and
"the new song."

KING OF GLORY

T. C. Horton and Charles E. Hurlburt

Who is this King of glory?
The LORD of hosts, he is the King of glory.

PSALM 24:10

*J*ehovah Jesus, the glorious King! Not merely a king but glorious, excelling all others in mighty truth and power, grace, and love. We almost forget for a time His absolute sovereignty as we bow in humble worship before His matchless glory, and cry again and again, "Thy Kingdom come," Oh Glorious King. Amen.

ACTS OF FREEDOM

Brother Lawrence

Now the Lord is that Spirit: and where the
Spirit of the Lord is, there is liberty.

2 CORINTHIANS 3:17

*W*hen we are faithful to keep ourselves in His holy presence and set Him always before us, this not only hinders our offending Him and doing anything that may displease Him, at least willfully, but it also begets in us a holy freedom; and, if I may so speak a familiarity with God, wherewith we ask, and that successfully, the graces we stand in need of. In time, by often repeating these acts, they become habitual, and the presence of God rendered as it were natural to us. Give Him thanks, if you please, with me, for His great goodness toward me, which I can never sufficiently admire, for the many favors He has done to so miserable a sinner as I am.

May all things praise Him. Amen.

BLESS THE LORD

Samuel Bagster

Because your love is better than life, my lips will glorify you.
I will praise you as long as I live. . . .

PSALM 63:3–4 NIV

*B*less the LORD, O my soul: and all that is within me, bless His holy name. Bless the LORD, O my soul, and forget not all His benefits" (Psalm 103:1 KJV). "I will bless the LORD at all times: His praise shall continually be in my mouth" (Psalm 34:1). "Every day will I bless Thee; and I will praise Thy name for ever and ever" (Psalm 145:2).

"Because Thy lovingkindness is better than life, my lips shall praise Thee. Thus will I bless Thee while I live: I will lift up my hands in Thy name. My soul shall be satisfied as with marrow and fatness; and my mouth shall praise Thee with joyful lips" (Psalm 63:3–5). "My soul doth magnify the Lord, and my spirit hath rejoiced in God my Saviour" (Luke 1:46–47).

"Thou art worthy, O Lord, to receive glory and honour and power: for Thou hast created all things, and for Thy pleasure they are and were created" (Revelation 4:11).

O Come Let Us Adore Him

Mrs. Charles E. Cowman

And they shall call his name Emmanuel. . .God with us.
MATTHEW 1:23

A striking Christmas card was published with the title, "If Christ had not come." The card represented a clergyman falling into a short sleep in his study on Christmas morning and dreaming of a world into which Jesus had never come.

A ring at the doorbell, and a messenger asked him to visit a poor, dying mother. He hastened with the weeping child, and as he reached the home he sat down and said, "I have something here that will comfort you." He opened his Bible to look for a familiar promise, but it ended at Malachi, and there was no gospel and no promise of hope and salvation, and he could only bow his head and weep with her in bitter despair.

Two days afterward he stood beside her coffin and conducted the funeral service, but there was no message of consolation, no word of a glorious resurrection, no open heaven, but only "dust to dust, ashes to ashes," and one long, eternal farewell. He realized at length that "He had not" and burst into tears and bitter weeping in his sorrowful dream.

Suddenly he woke with a start, and a great shout of joy and praise burst from his lips as he heard his choir singing in his church close by.

Let us be glad and rejoice today, because "He has come."

THE JOY OF THE LORD

from *Daily Strength for Daily Needs*

Let the hearts of those who seek the LORD rejoice.

PSALM 105:3 NIV

Be Thou my Sun, my selfishness destroy,
Thy atmosphere of Love be all my joy;
Thy Presence be my sunshine ever bright,
My soul the little mote that lives
but in Thy light.

GERHARD TERSTEEGEN

I do not know when I have had happier times in my soul than when I have been sitting at work with nothing before me but a candle and a white cloth, and hearing no sound but that of my own breath, with God in my soul and heaven in my eye. . . . I rejoice in being exactly what I am—a creature capable of loving God, and who, as long as God lives, must be happy. I get up and look for a while out of the window and gaze at the moon and stars, the work of an Almighty hand. I think of the grandeur of the universe and then sit down and think myself one of the happiest beings in it.

A POOR, 18TH-CENTURY METHODIST WOMAN

Joy in the Valleys

❧

*Consider it pure joy, my brothers and sisters, whenever
you face trials of many kinds, because you know that
the testing of your faith produces perseverance.*

JAMES 1:2–3 NIV

ARTIST AT WORK

R. T. Kendall

...to be conformed to the image of his Son...
ROMANS 8:29

A sculptor was going to make a horse out of a big block of marble and somebody came along to him and said, "How are you going to do that?"

He replied, "It's simple. I just start chipping away, and I chip away anything that doesn't look like a horse!"

And so with us. God takes the big block we give Him. He begins to chip away anything that is not just like His Son. We have been predestined "to be conformed to the image of his Son" (Romans 8:29). The day will eventually come when He can begin to use us.

The reason God lets us suffer is to chip away what isn't like Jesus, otherwise we will keep on making the same old mistakes. We may say, "Why do I do that all the time?" Perhaps it is because we haven't yet submitted ourselves to God's refining fires. This is why James said, "Count it all joy when ye fall into divers temptations" (James 1:2). May I suggest this: The next time a trial comes, rather than battle it out, rather than try to be rid of it and grumble the whole time, accept it graciously. See what God does.

THE STRENGTH OF MY HEART
Mrs. Charles E. Cowman

*"Whoever drinks the water I
give them will never thirst."*

JOHN 4:14 NIV

My heart needs Thee, O Lord, my heart needs Thee! No part of my being needs Thee like my heart. All else within me can be filled by Thy gifts. My hunger can be satisfied by daily bread. My thirst can be allayed by earthly waters. My cold can be removed by household fires. My weariness can be relieved by outward rest. But no outward thing can make my heart pure. The calmest day will not calm my passions. The fairest scene will not beautify my soul. The richest music will not make harmony within. The breezes can cleanse the air, but no breeze can cleanse a spirit. This world has not provided for my heart. It has provided for my eye; it has provided for my ear; it has provided for my touch; it has provided for my taste; it has provided for my sense of beauty; but it has not provided for my heart.

Lift up your eyes unto the hills! Make haste to Calvary, "Calvary's awful mountain climb," and on the way there visit the slopes of Mount Olive, where grow the trees of Gethsemane. Contemplate there the agony of the Lord, where He already tasted the tremendous cup, which He drank to the dregs the next noontide on the Cross. There is the answer to your need.

BENT ON KINDNESS
Hannah Whitall Smith

For I know the thoughts that I think toward you, saith the LORD, thoughts of peace, and not of evil, to give you an expected end.

JEREMIAH 29:11

A great many people are afraid of the consuming fire of God, but that is only because they do not understand what it is. It is the fire of God's love that must in the very nature of things consume everything that can harm His people; and if our hearts are set on being what the love of God would have us to be, His fire is something we shall not be afraid of but shall warmly welcome.

> *Implacable is love.*
> *Foes may be bought or teased*
> *From their malign intent;*
> *But he goes unappeased,*
> *Who is on kindness bent.*

Fear Not

from *Daily Strength for Daily Needs*

Stormy winds that do his bidding...
PSALM 148:8 NIV

Stormy winds come not without mercy and blessing. There is music in the blast if we listen aright. Is there no music in the heart of sorrow that the Lord of all has chosen for His own? Are you not nearer to the Master, have you not grown in faith, in patience, in prayerfulness, in thankful hope, since the time the storm winds first sighed across your life?

Do not tremble because of the winds of the future; your Lord will be living and loving tomorrow, even as He lives and loves today, and no storm waits in your path but shall leave behind another record that your heavenly Father is stronger than the tempest, nearer than the grief.

We are traveling home to that beauteous shore where the chill winds never sweep, the hurricane makes no moan; yet, amid the rest of the painless Homeland, shall we not love the Lord a thousandfold more for every storm of earth in which He drew near to us, saying, "Fear not," and held us by the hand and tenderly bore us through the hour that seemed the darkest? We shall glorify Him then that He has been to us, again and again, a cover from the blast, but let us not wait to glorify Him till the blast is over.

Trials Make Room for Consolation

Charles H. Spurgeon

❦

For as the sufferings of Christ abound in us,
so our consolation also aboundeth by Christ.

2 Corinthians 1:5

Here is a blessed proportion. The Ruler of Providence bears a pair of scales—in this side He puts His people's trials, and in that He puts their consolations. When the scale of trial is nearly empty, you will find the scale of consolation just as heavy. When the black clouds gather most, the light is the more brightly revealed on us. When the night lowers and the tempest is coming on, the Heavenly Captain is always closest to His crews. It is a blessed thing that when we are most cast down, then it is that we are most lifted up by the consolations of the Spirit. One reason is because trials make more room for consolation. Great hearts can only be made by great troubles. . . . God comes into our heart—He finds it full—He begins to break our comforts and to make it empty; then there is more room for grace. The humbler a man lies, the more comfort he will always have, because he will be more fitted to receive it.

Come, troubled believer, fret not over your heavy troubles, for they are the herald of weighty mercies.

ENDURANCE

Mrs. Charles E. Cowman

*"But he knows the way that I take; when he
has tested me, I will come forth as gold."*

JOB 23:10 NIV

A number of years ago, I knew a woman who found God to be a very wonderful Friend. She had a rich Christian experience, but there came into her life a very great trial: Her home was broken up; the crash was unspeakable; in the midst of it all, it seemed that the Father forsook her.

One evening after prayer-meeting, she arose and gave this testimony. We all knew how precious God was to her. Her face was pale and thin. She had suffered much. "God and I have been such wonderful friends, but He seems very far away. He seems to have withdrawn Himself from me. I seem to be left utterly alone." Then looking off in the distance, and with tears, she continued, "But if I never see His face again, I will keep looking at the spot where I saw His face last."

I have never seen nor heard of anything finer than that. That is mighty, sublime, glorious faith that keeps going on. There is a wonderful outcome to the trials in a life of victorious faith like this. This was Job's greatest triumph. "He knoweth the way that I take. The Lord gave and the Lord hath taken away. Blessed be the Name of the Lord."

DEAN DUTTON

FEELING OUR INFIRMITIES
R. T. Kendall

*We have not an high priest which cannot be touched
with the feeling of our infirmities; but was in all
points tempted like as we are, yet without sin.*

HEBREWS 4:15

*G*od feels a thousand times more deeply than we do for
ourselves. This is the way Jesus feels behind the scenes.
"We have not an high priest which cannot be touched
with the feeling of our infirmities; but was in all points
tempted like as we are, yet without sin" (Hebrews 4:15).
Our Lord is touched with the feeling of our weaknesses.
It doesn't only mean that He used to be touched when
He was on earth, as if that the only time He could
sympathize. It describes how Jesus feels right now. He
yearns to reveal Himself now. And yet He is bound to
certain principles. One of those principles is described
in Acts 14:22, "We must through much tribulation enter
into the kingdom of God." But in the meantime He feels
what we feel—only a thousand times more. Our Lord
weeps with us now. He weeps because of what He sees
that we don't see; for He has much more to feel deeply
about than we have.

> *Standing somewhere in the shadows you'll find Jesus,*
> *He's the Friend who always cares and understands.*
> *Standing somewhere in the shadows you will find Him,*
> *And you'll know Him by the nailprints in His hands.*

KEEP YOUR EYES ON JESUS

Ken Abraham

*For I know the thoughts that I think toward you, saith the LORD,
thoughts of peace, and not of evil, to give you an expected end.*

JEREMIAH 29:11

You may be experiencing terribly difficult days. He may be bringing you through a desperately demanding period in your life or through a dry, dusty wilderness. Possibly you have been humiliated as you have struggled to hold onto your faith in an entirely new or unfamiliar set of circumstances.

Keep your eyes on Jesus! You've probably been tempted to stick your head up, gawk around, and say, "Lord, what about him (or her)? God, this is not fair! You know I love you. Now, what's all this about?"

Perhaps you have been tempted to look across the aisle at church, or across the street from where you live, or maybe even across your dining room table, and think, *Lord, why aren't You dealing with that person the way You are turning the heat up on me? Why do they have it so cozy and comfortable?*

If you listen carefully, you will probably hear the Spirit of Jesus say, "What is that to you? You follow me!"

Understand, God is not calling everyone to do what He has called you to do. He is working in each one of our lives in wonderfully different ways, so each of us can magnify and glorify the name of Jesus.

BEAUTY FROM UGLINESS

Mrs. Charles E. Cowman

*For we which live are always delivered unto death
for Jesus' sake, that the life also of Jesus might be
made manifest in our mortal flesh.*

2 CORINTHIANS 4:11

*E*very phase of nature about us is a wonder. Beauty
from ugliness, good out of evil, everywhere. The rose
sucks its life from some festering death beneath the sod.
The white pond-lily climbs up out of the muddy waters
and lifts its pure petals above slime and corruption. The
fleece-cloud of the upper heaven is the evaporation of
stagnant pools and swamps.

And in the human sphere, the most beautiful
lives are the outcome of anguish and tears. Then may
we not say, "We glory in tribulations; knowing that
tribulation worketh patience; and patience, experience;
and experience, hope." The rose of life as well as of the
garden, the sweet-scented flowers though they climb up
to such a height as to overrun the jasper walls, and bloom
fairest from the root of some death or loss, and grow
strong as they are shaken by the sharp winds of sorrow.

A PALACE FOR GOD

Ken Abraham

*Jesus replied, "Anyone who loves me will obey my teaching.
My Father will love them, and we will come
to them and make our home with them."*

JOHN 14:23 NIV

*W*riter C. S. Lewis knew well the temptations to judge
ourselves and each other by false standards. He also
understood the balance between our perseverance and
God's patience with our imperfections:

"On the one hand, God's demand for perfection
need not discourage you in the least in your present
attempts to be good or even perfect in your present
failures. On the other hand, you must realize from the
outset that the goal toward which He is beginning to
guide you is absolute perfection; and no power in the
whole universe, except you yourself, can prevent Him
from taking you to the goal."

Borrowing from George MacDonald, another great
writer, Lewis continued, "Imagine yourself as a living
house. God comes in to rebuild that house. At first,
perhaps, you can understand what He is doing. But
presently He starts knocking the house about in a way
that hurts abominably and does not seem to make sense.

"You thought you were going to be made into a
decent little cottage, but He is building a palace. He
intends to come and live in it Himself. If you think that
you don't deserve God's grace, you are right. But then
again, neither do the rest of us."

IN GETHSEMANE

John Henry Jowett

And when he was at the place, he said unto them,
Pray that ye enter not into temptation.

LUKE 22:40

Surely this is the very Holy of Holies! It is well for us to fall on our knees and "be silent unto the Lord." I would quietly listen to the awful words, "Remove this cup from Me!" and I would listen again and again until never again do I hold a cheap religion. It is in this garden that we learn the real value of things and come to know the price at which our redemption was bought. No one can remain in Gethsemane and retain a frivolous and flippant spirit.

"And there appeared unto Him an angel from heaven, strengthening Him." I know that angel! He has been to me. He has brought me angel's food, even heavenly manna. Always and everywhere when my soul has surrendered itself to the Divine will, the angel comes, and my soul is refreshed. The laying down of self is the taking up of God. When I lose my will, I gain the Infinite. The moment of surrender is also the moment of conquest. When I consecrate my weakness, I put on strength and majesty like a robe. "And when He rose up from His prayer"—what then? Just this, He was quietly ready for anything, ready for the betraying kiss, ready for crucifixion. "Arise, let us be going."

THE CROWN OF THORNS

Mrs. Charles E. Cowman

"Instead of the thorn shall come up the fir tree, and instead of the brier shall come up the myrtle tree: and it shall be to the LORD for a name, for an everlasting sign that shall not be cut off."

ISAIAH 55:13

*A*n old legend relates that long ago some monks had found a crown of thorns which the Savior wore on the day He was crucified. During Passion Week it was laid on the altar of the chapel, and the people looked upon the sacred crown with great reverence, awed as they saw the cruel thorns still bearing their stains of blood.

Very early on Easter morning, one of the monks entered the chapel to remove the relic which would be so out of harmony with the glad thoughts of the day. When he opened the door, he found the whole place filled with wondrous perfume. He could not understand it. As he went up to the altar, the early sunlight, coming in through the eastern window, showed him the crown still resting there, but it had become a crown of roses, every rose pouring out its marvelous fragrance.

The beautiful legend is a parable of what Christ does with earth's sorrows for all who love and trust Him. Out of pain comes blessing. The crown of thorns must be worn by the Master's own, but the thorns burst into sweet flowers as the light of heaven's morning touches them.

WINGS OF EAGLES
Hannah Whitall Smith

They will soar on wings like eagles.
ISAIAH 40:31 NIV

It is not worthwhile to cry out, "Oh that I had wings and then I would flee," for we have the wings already, and what is needed is not more wings but only that we should use those we have. The power to surrender and trust exists in every human soul and only needs to be brought into exercise. With these two wings we can "flee" to God at any moment, but in order really to reach Him, we must actively use them. We must not merely want to use them, but we must do it definitely and actively. We shall not "mount up" very high if we only surrender and trust in theory or in our especially religious moments. We must do it definitely and practically about each detail of daily life as it comes to us. We must meet our disappointments, our thwartings, our persecutions, our malicious enemies, our provoking friends, our trials and temptations of every sort, with an active and experimental attitude of surrender and trust. We must spread our wings and "mount up" to the "heavenly places in Christ" above them all, where they will lose their power to harm or distress us. For from these high places we shall see things through the eye of Christ, and all earth will be glorified in the heavenly vision.

THE CAPTAIN OF
OUR SALVATION

T. C. Horton and Charles E. Hurlbut

*It was fitting that God. . .should make the pioneer of
their salvation perfect through what he suffered.*

HEBREWS 2:10 NIV

*W*e cannot but bow our heads as we read this verse
and meditate upon the Captain of our salvation and
His perfection. He was God and He was Man, we have
learned. As Man He must be manifest in the life. He is
the Son of God, the Captain (or "Author") of salvation.
We are the sons of God. The mode and method of
perfection is manifested by our Leader. He was tempted;
so are we. He suffered; so must we. He was persecuted;
so must we be. He paid the price; so must we. The
climax for Him and for us is glory. Let us bow our heads
and hearts to our Leader today and obey His orders. He
will be with us in every trial and suffering. Amen.

WE'RE IN FOR A FIGHT

Ken Abraham

*Put on the whole armour of God, that ye may
be able to stand against the wiles of the devil.*

EPHESIANS 6:11

To be a Christian means that we are involved in a war,
a spiritual war between God's people and the forces
of Satan. We are at war with evil, a personal evil, a
supernatural evil, spearheaded by Satan himself. The
devil is not some funny-looking cartoon character with
horns sticking out of his head, dressed in red leotards,
and carrying a pitchfork. No, the devil is real, and he is
your enemy. He has sent his demonic messengers into
the world to stand against you and do all they can to
keep you from being the person God wants you to be.

The war is raging in cities and towns all across the
land. Sadly, Satan is winning many victories. The devil
and demonic cohorts are ripping apart friends and family
relationships; they are splitting churches wide open,
sapping the life-blood out of many believers, and sucking
some of your friends and family members right down
into hell.

It's time to stand up and fight back! In the name of
Jesus, by the power of His Holy Spirit working in us, and
by the blood of the Lamb, it's time for each of us to tell
the devil where to get off. God is calling us out of our
complacency to become warriors for Christ.

Sickness among Christ's Friends

John Henry Jowett

*Lord, behold, he whom thou lovest is sick. When Jesus heard that,
he said, This sickness is not unto death, but for the glory of God,
that the Son of God might be glorified thereby.*

JOHN 11:3–4

*A*nd so sickness can enter the circle of the friends of
the Lord. "He whom Thou lovest is sick." My sicknesses
do not mean that I have lost His favor. The shadow is
His, as well as the sunshine. When He removes from
the glare of boisterous health it may be because of some
spiritual fern which needs the ministry of the shade.
"This sickness is. . .for the glory of God." Something
beautiful will spring out of the shadowed seclusion,
something which shall spread abroad the name and fame
of God.

And, therefore, I do not wonder at the Lord's delay.
We are impatient to get healthy; the Lord desires that we
become holy. Our physical sickness is continued in order
that we may put on spiritual strength.

And there are others besides sick Lazarus concerned
in the sickness: "I am glad for your sakes I was not
there." The disciples were included in the divine scheme.
Their spiritual welfare was to be affected by it. Let me
ever remember that the circle affected by sickness is
always wider than the patient's bed. And may God be
glorified in all!

God Enlightens My Darkness

from *Daily Strength for Daily Needs*

My God turns my darkness into light.

PSALM 18:28 NIV

When we in darkness walk,
Nor feel the heavenly flame,
Then is the time to trust our God,
And rest upon His name.

A. M. TOPLADY

*H*e has an especial tenderness of love toward thee for that thou art in the dark and hast no light, and His heart is glad when thou dost arise and say, "I will go to my Father." For He sees thee through all the gloom through which thou canst not see Him. Say to Him, "My God, I am very dull and low and hard; but Thou are wise and high and tender, and Thou art my God. I am Thy child. Forsake me not." Then fold the arms of thy faith and wait in quietness until light goes up in the darkness. Fold the arms of thy Faith, I say, but not of thy Action: Bethink thee of something that thou oughtest to do, and go and do it, if it be but the sweeping of a room or the preparing of a meal or a visit to a friend, heed not thy feelings; do thy work.

GEORGE MACDONALD

GOD IS ENOUGH

Hannah Whitall Smith

Train up a child in the way he should go:
and when he is old, he will not depart from it.

PROVERBS 22:6

The all-sufficiency of God ought to be as complete to the child of God as the all-sufficiency of a good mother is to the child of that mother. We all know the utter rest of the little child in the mother's presence and the mother's love. That its mother is there is enough to make all fears and all troubles disappear. It does not need the mother to make any promises; she herself, just as she is, without promises and without explanations, is all that the child needs.

My mother was the remedy for all my own ills, and, I fully believed, for the ills of the whole world, if only they could be brought to her. And when anyone expressed doubts as to her capacity to remedy everything, I remembered with what fine scorn I used to annihilate them by saying, "Ah! But you don't know my mother."

And now, when any tempest-tossed soul fails to see that God is enough, I feel like saying, not with scorn but with infinite pity, "Ah, dear friend, you do not know God! Did you know Him, you could not help seeing that He is the remedy for every need of your soul and that He is an all-sufficient remedy. God is enough."

LOOK UP!

F. B. Meyer

*And when these things begin to come to pass, then look up,
and lift up your heads; for your redemption draweth nigh.*

LUKE 21:28

*E*ach great crisis in the past has helped to advance
the glorious reign of Christ. Was the fall of Babylon a
crisis? It gave mankind a universal speech—the language
spoken by Alexander and his soldiers—the delicate,
subtle Greek in which the New Testament was written.
Was the fall of Rome a crisis? It opened the way to
the rise of the northern nations, which have ever been
the home of Liberty and the gospel. Was the fall of
feudalism, in the French Revolution, a crisis? It made
the splendid achievements of the nineteenth century
possible. And we may look without dismay on events
that cast a shadow on our hearts. They also shall serve
the cause of the gospel. In ways we cannot tell, they shall
prepare for the triumph of our King. Through the throes
of the present travail, the new heavens and earth shall be
born. The agony is not as the expiring groan of the dying
gladiator but as the sigh of the mother bringing forth her
firstborn. These things, said our Lord, must needs be;
and they are the beginning of travail (see Matthew 24:8).
And amid all, Jesus rides in triumph to His destined
glory and the crown of all the earth.

Joy in Who God Is

*For the L*ORD *your God is God of gods and*
Lord of lords, the great God, mighty and awesome.

DEUTERONOMY 10:17 NIV

HE IS WISDOM

Jill Briscoe

Christ. . .has become for us wisdom from God. . . .
1 CORINTHIANS 1:30 NIV

$\mathcal{T}$he earthly king and queen of Hearts in Proverbs knew very well that "the fear of the LORD is the beginning of knowledge" (Proverbs 1:7). The King of Hearts in heaven promises an ongoing revelation of wisdom because He is wisdom, and is a giving God. "Christ. . .is made unto us wisdom. . . ." (1 Corinthians 1:30), Paul tells us. That ongoing revelation will never stop. What's more, He promises that what we know of Him down here is only the beginning. "Eye hath not seen, nor ear heard, neither have entered into the heart of man, the things which God hath prepared for them that love him," He promises in 1 Corinthians 2:9. That's why eternity will be so necessary. That's how long it's going to take to know all there is to know about our wise and wonderful heavenly King of Hearts. "The fear of the LORD is clean, enduring for ever. . . ," sings the psalmist in [Psalm] 19:9.

Yes, wisdom lasts forever.

THE LIVING CHRIST

Andrew Murray

"But when he, the Spirit of truth comes,
he will guide you into all the truth."

JOHN 16:13 NIV

The Holy Spirit was given for this one purpose—that the glorious redemption and life in Christ might with divine power be conveyed and communicated to us. We have the Holy Spirit to make the living Christ, in all His saving power and in the completeness of His victory over sin, ever present within us. It is this that constitutes Him the Comforter: With Him we need never mourn an absent Christ. Let us therefore, as often as we read or meditate or pray in connection with this abiding in Christ, reckon upon it as a settled thing that we have the Spirit of God Himself within us, teaching and guiding and working. Let us rejoice in the confidence that we must succeed in our desires, because the Holy Spirit is working all the while with secret but divine power in the soul that does not hinder Him by its unbelief.

God Manifested
in the Flesh

T. C. Horton and Charles E. Hurlburt

And without controversy great is the mystery of godliness: God was manifest in the flesh, justified in the Spirit, seen of angels, preached unto the Gentiles, believed on in the world, received up into glory.

1 Timothy 3:16

*H*ere is a sermon of marvelous mystery. In a few words we are given the magnitude of the mission of Christ in leaving the glory and coming to this earth, clothed in the garments of flesh; accomplishing His divine mission of redemption while in human form; leaving His witnesses to His crucifixion, resurrection, and ascension to His high and holy place in glory. We should stand with uncovered heads and with hearts beating in adoration, worshipping Him as the Holy Spirit of God emphasizes to us this great truth: He came, He died, He lives in us and He lives in glory, and we will dwell forever with Him.

Holy Spirit, help us to magnify and glorify God.
Amen.

Messiah

T. C. Horton and Charles E. Hurlburt

The woman said, "I know that Messiah" (called Christ)
"is coming. When he comes, he will explain everything to us."
JOHN 4:25 NIV

*T*here is no book like the Bible and there never can be. Christ's interview with the woman at the well and His revelation of Himself is unique and contrary to any conception that could have been made of Him. The Samaritans, as did the Jews, anticipated a Christ (an anointed One). This was the promise given in Deuteronomy 18:18. This woman was the last one we would have chosen for such a revelation—but her soul was filled at once with the Spirit of life and hope, and her lips bore a testimony—humiliating to herself—but bringing salvation to a multitude. Oh, that our lips might bear such convincing, convicting, and converting testimony.

Lord, make us like this Samaritan woman! Amen.

A Friend That Sticketh Closer Than a Brother

T. C. Horton and Charles E. Hurlburt

A man that hath friends must shew himself friendly:
and there is a friend that sticketh closer than a brother.
PROVERBS 18:24

Stay, lonely pilgrim, searching long for fellowship. Stop here and find "A Friend."

"There is a Friend," though all the world deny it. One who is always true and faithful. One who never leaves and ne'er forsakes. No brother will, or can, abide as He. Will you be a friend to Jesus, as He is a friend to thee?

We worship Thee, we trust all to Thee, and take from Thee all peace,
all grace, all needed power to do and be what pleaseth Thee,
our never-absent Friend. Amen.

GOD

T. C. Horton and Charles E. Hurlburt

But unto the Son he saith, Thy throne,
O God, is for ever and ever.

HEBREWS 1:8

*H*ere we have the Alpine height in titles for our Lord, "Thy throne, O God!" All other names and titles are inferior to this. When He was born in a manger, God was there. When He worked at the carpenter's trade, God was there at work. When He associated with the fishermen, it was God who was their companion.

When He spoke, God spoke. When He died on the cross, it was God Himself who poured out His life. When He comes "with a shout," it will be the voice of God that calls us to be with Him forever. It is God the Son who holds the sceptre and rules the worlds, and we will rule and reign with Him.

Oh, God our Savior and coming King, hasten Thy coming, and help us to help Thee hasten that day, for Thine own name's sake. Amen.

When God Says "Thank You"

Jill Briscoe

His lord said unto him, Well done, thou good and faithful servant:
thou hast been faithful over a few things, I will make thee ruler
over many things: enter thou into the joy of thy lord.

MATTHEW 25:21

*M*ost of our lives we concentrate on the fact that we must affirm our faith in God and appreciate Him. It's quite different to think of God affirming His faith in us and appreciating us. It's a new concept for many of us that He can be pleased with us at all! But it's a good concept! Once a human being has been on his knees and felt the hand of God upon his head in praise, he will never be the same again. There is nothing that makes you feel quite so loved, warm, and complete as when God says, "Thank you." No matter if all the world rejects you—His word of affirmation is enough. We must learn to live our lives looking for that word.

THE CRUCIED ONE

Andrew Murray

*I have been crucified with Christ and
I no longer live, but Christ lives in me.*

GALATIANS 2:20 NIV

"I am crucified with Christ." Thus the apostle expresses his assurance of his fellowship with Christ in His sufferings and death and his full participation in all the power and the blessing of that death. And so really did he mean what he said, and know that he was now indeed dead, that he adds "It is no longer I that live, but Christ that liveth in me." How blessed must be the experience of such a union with the Lord Jesus! To be able to look upon His death as mine, just as it was His—upon His perfect obedience to God, His victory over sin, and complete deliverance from its power, as mine; and to realize that the power of that death does by faith work daily with a divine energy in mortifying the flesh, and renewing the whole life into the perfect conformity to the resurrection life of Jesus! Abiding in Jesus, the Crucified One, is the secret of the growth of that new life which is ever begotten of the death of nature.

The Rock of My Salvation

T. C. Horton and Charles E. Hurlburt

The LORD liveth; and blessed be my rock;
and exalted be the God of the rock of my salvation.

2 SAMUEL 22:47

*N*o graver danger threatens the believer than that of forgetting that he was redeemed—forgetting even in the joy of realized life what our salvation cost and what is the rock foundation of our faith. To meet this need, our Savior pictures Himself not merely as the Rock of Ages and our Strong Rock of Refuge but the Rock of our Salvation. Here, in Him and upon His merit and atoning grace, we were saved from among the lost. Let us glory in this precious name and never forget that He was "wounded for our transgressions" and "that He bore our sins in His own body on the tree."

My Own Shepherd

John Henry Jowett

The LORD is my shepherd;
I shall not want.

PSALM 23:1

*H*ow shall we touch this lovely psalm and not bruise it? It is exquisite as "a violet by a mossy stone"! Exposition is almost an impertinence, its grace is so simple and winsome.

There is the ministry of rest. "He maketh me to lie down in green pastures." The Good Shepherd knows when my spirit needs relaxation. He will not have me always "on the stretch." The bow of the best violin sometimes requires having its strings "let down," and so my Lord gives me rest.

And there is the discipline of change. "He leadeth me in the paths of righteousness." Those strange roads in life, unknown roads, by which I pass into changed circumstances and surroundings! But the discipline of the change is only to bring me into new pastures, that I may gain fresh nutriment for my soul. "Because they have no changes, they fear not God."

And there is "the valley of the shadow," cold and bare! What matter? He is there! "I will fear no evil." What if I see "no pastures green"? "Thy rod and thy staff they comfort me!" The Lord, who is leading, will see after my food. "Thou preparest a table before me in the presence of mine enemies." I have a quiet feast while my foes are looking on!

RESTORER

T. C. Horton and Charles E. Hurlburt

*He refreshes my soul. He guides me along
the right paths for his name's sake.*

PSALM 23:3 NIV

*W*e wander from God and from the paths of
righteousness—from following Him beside the still
waters—till we lose the way, lose joy, lose the sound of
His voice. Then the Master "restoreth (the only use of
this form in the Old Testament) our soul," "brings us
back into His Way," into the paths of righteousness.

*Oh, gracious "Restorer," bring back my wandering soul
as a straying sheep, and lead me on in the paths of
righteousness "for Thy name's sake." Amen.*

PARDONING FORGIVENESS

Andrew Murray

Lord, how oft shall. . .I forgive him? . . .
Jesus saith unto him. . . Until seventy times seven.
MATTHEW 18:21–22

*W*e pray, "Forgive, even as we have forgiven." Scripture
says, "Forgive one another, even as God also in Christ
forgave you." God's full and free forgiveness is to be
the rule of ours with men. Otherwise our reluctant,
halfhearted forgiveness, which is not forgiveness at all,
will be God's rule with us. Every prayer rests upon our
faith in God's pardoning grace. If God dealt with us
after our sins, not one prayer could be heard. Pardon
opens the door to all God's love and blessing: Because
God has pardoned all our sins, our prayer can prevail
to obtain all we need. The deep, sure ground of answer
to prayer is God's forgiving love. When it has taken
possession of the heart, we pray in faith. But also, when
it has taken possession of the heart, we live in love. God's
forgiving disposition, revealed in His love to us, becomes
a disposition in us; as the power of His forgiving love
shed abroad and dwelling within us, we forgive even as
He forgives.

"I Am" Is the Same
Hannah Whitall Smith

He that hath seen me hath seen the Father. . . .
JOHN 14:9

It is unthinkable to suppose that when God told Moses His name was "I am," He could have meant to say, "I am a stern Lawgiver," or "I am a hard Taskmaster," or "I am a God who is wrapped up in my own glory and am indifferent to the sorrows or the fears of my people." If we should try to fill in the blank of His "I am" with such things as these, all the Christians the world over would be horrified. But do not the doubts and fears of some of these very Christians say exactly these things in secret every day of their lives?

May God grant that what we shall learn in our consideration of the names of God may make all such doubts and fears impossible to us from this time forth and forevermore.

Jesus is God! Oh, could I now
But compass land and sea,
To teach and tell this single truth,
How happy I should be!
Oh, had I but an angel's voice,
I would proclaim so loud
Jesus, the good, the beautiful,
Is the image of our God!

Assuming a Promise

Ken Abraham

God had power to do what he had promised.

ROMANS 4:21 NIV

Abraham assumed he was walking in the center of God's will for his life. But by taking things into his own hands, Abraham was soon to learn one of the most difficult lessons a child of God can learn. God let him wander in the wilderness of his own mistakes for the next thirteen years!

For thirteen years, it seemed to Abraham that the heavens were brass. Worse still, during that entire time, Abraham probably thought he was in the will of God! How painful it must have been for him to discover that he had been so deluded.

God was teaching Abraham an important lesson: When a child of God takes things into his or her own hands and attempts to manipulate people, relationships, or situations, God will allow him to do it. He may not even say a word. Then He will allow His child to struggle through the darkness and foolishness he or she has created.

If you have learned the lesson God has been trying to teach you through delays and detours, you will probably be more than ready to listen to him the next time He speaks. That's what happened in Abraham's life, and the next word he received from God was the promise that within a year their long-awaited son would be born. . .and God kept His promise.

THE PRICE OF SIN

Charles H. Spurgeon

With his stripes we are healed.

ISAIAH 53:5

*P*ilate delivered our Lord to the lictors to be scourged. The Roman scourge was a most dreadful instrument of torture. It was made of the sinews of oxen, and sharp bones were intertwined here and there among the sinews so that every time the lash came down, these pieces of bone inflicted fearful lacerations and tore off the flesh from the bone. The Savior was, no doubt, bound to the column and thus beaten. He had been beaten before, but this beating with the Roman lictors was probably the most severe of His flagellations.

Believer in Jesus, can you gaze upon Him without tears as He stands before you the mirror of agonizing love? He is at once fair as the lily of innocence and red as the rose with the crimson of His own blood. As we feel the sure and blessed healing which His stripes have wrought in us, do not our hearts melt at once with love and grief? If ever we have loved our Lord Jesus, surely we must feel that affection glowing now within our bosoms.

See how the patient Jesus stands,
Insulted in His lowest case!
Sinners have bound the Almighty's hands,
And spit in their Creator's face.
With thorns His temples gor'd and gash'd
Send streams of blood from every part;
His back's with knotted scourges lash'd
But sharper sources tear His heart.

My Share in the Miracle

John Henry Jowett

His mother saith unto the servants,
Whatsoever he saith unto you, do it.

JOHN 2:5

*O*ur Lord always demands our best. He will not work with our second best. His gracious "extra" is given when our own resources are exhausted. We must do our best before our Master will do His miracle. We must "fill the water-pots with water"! We must bring "the five loaves and two fishes"! We must "let down the net"! We must be willing "to be made whole," and we must make the effort to rise! Yes, the Lord will have my best.

Our Lord transforms our best into His better. He changes water into wine. He turns the handful of seed into a harvest. Our aspirations become inspirations. Our willingness becomes magnetic with the mystic power of grace. Our bread becomes sacramental, and He Himself reveals to us at the feast. Our ordinary converse becomes a Divine fellowship, and "our hearts burn within us" as He talks to us by the way.

And our Lord ever keeps His best wine until the last. "Eye hath not seen, nor ear heard, neither hath it entered into the heart of man, the things which God hath prepared for them that love Him" (1 Corinthians 2:9).

THE GREATEST MIRACLE

James Stalker

At that very time Jesus who had cured many diseases,
sicknesses and evil spirits.

LUKE 7:21 NIV

The miracles of Christ were the natural outflow of
the divine fullness which dwelt in Him. God was in
Him, and His human nature was endowed with the
Holy Ghost without measure. It was natural, when such
a Being was in the world, that mighty works should
manifest themselves in Him. He was Himself the great
miracle, of which His particular miracles were merely
sparks or emanations. He was the great interruption of
the order of nature, or rather a new element which had
entered into the order of nature to enrich and ennoble it,
and His miracles entered with Him, not to disturb but
to repair its harmony. Therefore all His miracles bore the
stamp of His character. They were not mere exhibitions
of power, but also of holiness, wisdom, and love.

Joy in Love

❧

"A new command I give you: Love one another.
As I have loved you, so you must love one another.
By this everyone will know that you are my disciples,
if you love one another."

JOHN 13:34-35 NIV

Loving the Lord

John Henry Jowett

Whoever does not love does not know God,
because God is love.

1 John 4:8 niv

The secret of life is to love the Lord our God and our neighbors as ourselves. But how are we to love the Lord? We cannot manufacture love. We cannot love to order. We cannot by an act of will command its appearing. No, not in these ways is love created. Love is not a work, it is a fruit. It grows in suitable soils, and it is our part to prepare the soils. When the conditions are congenial, love appears, just as the crocus and the snowdrop appear in the congenial air of the spring.

What, then, can we do? We can think about Him. We can read about Him. We can fill our imaginations with the grace of His life and service. We can be much with Him, talking to Him in prayer, singing to Him in praise, telling Him our yearnings and confessing to Him our defeats. And love will be quietly born. For this is how love is born between heart and heart. Two people are "much together," and love is born! And when we are much with the Lord, we are with One who already loves us with an everlasting love. We are with One who yearns because He first loved us. And when we truly love God, every other kind of holy love will follow. Given the fountain, the rivers are sure.

LOVE ONE ANOTHER

from *Daily Strength for Daily Needs*

If we love one another, God dwelleth in us,
and his love is perfected in us.

1 JOHN 4:12

Abide in me; o'ershadow by Thy love
Each half-formed purpose and dark thought of sin;
Quench, ere it rise, each selfish, low desire,
And keep my soul as Thine, calm and divine.

H. B. STOWE

The Spirit of love must work the works and speak the tones of Love. It cannot exist and give no sign or a false sign. It cannot be a spirit of Love and mantle into irritable and selfish impatience. It cannot be a spirit of Love and at the same time make self the prominent object. It cannot rejoice to lend itself to the happiness of others and at the same time be seeking its own. It cannot be generous and envious. It cannot be sympathizing and unseemly; self-forgetful and vainglorious. It cannot delight in the rectitude and purity of other hearts, as the spiritual elements of their peace, and yet unnecessarily suspect them.

J. H. THOM

Herein Is Love

Dietrich Bonhoeffer

But I say unto you which hear, Love your enemies,
do good to them which hate you.

LUKE 6:27

*B*y our enemies, Jesus means those who are quite
intractable and utterly unresponsive to our love, who
forgive us nothing when we forgive them all, who requite
our love with hatred and our service, with derision, "For
my love they are my adversaries: but I give myself unto
prayer" (Psalm 109:4). Love asks nothing in return but
seeks those who need it. And who needs our love more
than those who are consumed with hatred and are utterly
devoid of love? Who, in other words, deserves our love
more than our enemy? Where is love more glorified than
where she dwells in the midst of her enemies?

THE HOPE OF GLORY

Andrew Murray

Christ in you, the hope of glory.
COLOSSIANS 1:27

$\mathcal{A}$nd if the thought will sometimes come: Surely this is too high for us; can it be really true? Only remember that the greatness of the privilege is justified by the greatness of the object He has in view. Christ was the revelation of the Father on earth. He could not be this if there were not the most perfect unity, the most complete communication of all the Father had to the Son. He could be it because the Father loved Him and He abode in that love. Believers are the revelation of Christ on earth. They cannot be this unless there is perfect unity, so that the world can know that He loves them and has sent them. But they can be it if Christ loves them with the infinite love that gives itself and all it has and if they abide in that love.

THE JOY OF THE LOVER

John Henry Jowett

Be devoted to one another in love.
Honor one another above yourselves.

ROMANS 12:10 NIV

*L*ove finds her joy in seeing others crowned. Envy darkens when she sees the garland given to another. Jealousy has no festival except when she is "Queen of the May." But love thrills to another's exaltation. She feels the glow of another's triumph. When another basks in favor, her own "time of singing of birds is come"!

And all this is because love has wonderful chords which vibrate to the secret things in the souls of others. Indeed, the gift of love is just the gift of delicate correspondence, the power of exquisite fellow-feeling, the ability to "rejoice with them that do rejoice, and to weep with them that weep." When, therefore, the soul of another is exultant, and the wedding bells are ringing, love's kindred bells ring a merry peal. When the soul of another is depressed and a funeral dirge is wailing, love's kindred chords wail in sad communion. So love can enter another's state as though it were her own.

Our Master spake condemningly of those who have lost this exquisite gift. They have lost their power of response. "We have piped with you, and ye have not danced; we have mourned with you, and ye have not lamented." They lived in selfish and loveless isolation. They have lost all power of tender communion.

EXERCISING LOVE

Brother Lawrence

*But we all, with open face beholding as in a glass the glory
of the Lord, are changed into the same image from glory
to glory, even as by the Spirit of the Lord.*

2 CORINTHIANS 3:18

In the beginning of the spiritual life we ought to be
faithful in doing our duty and denying ourselves, but
after that, unspeakable pleasures follow. In difficulties
we need only have recourse to Jesus Christ and beg His
grace; with that everything became easy.

Many do not advance in the Christian progress
because they stick in penances and particular exercises,
while they neglect the love of God, which is the end.
This appeared plainly by their works and was the reason
why we see so little solid virtue. There needed neither art
nor science for going to God but only a heart resolutely
determined to apply itself to nothing but Him, or for
His sake, and to love Him only.

LOVE NEVER FAILS

Jill Briscoe

Love never fails.
1 CORINTHIANS 13:8 NIV

*L*ove cannot keep quiet. It has to tell of its love! The king of Hearts in Proverbs 31 praised his wife. He loved his queen so thoroughly, he delighted to tell her so, and He delights to tell us so.

Our heavenly King of Hearts is tender and sweet and precious. He knows how to make us feel like a million dollars when people tell us we're not worth a penny. He's written us a very long and beautiful love letter. It's called the Bible. What's more, we don't have to earn anything for His favor. We don't have to charm Him or pretend we are something we're not so He will like us. We don't have to compete with other women for His attention either. All we have to do is be still and know that He is God. Just be still enough—long enough—to be loved by His everlasting love. The love of God is shed abroad in a queen of Hearts' heart by the Holy Spirit, which is given unto us. "I love you; I love you; I love you"; the Spirit of the King whispers—and this when others are shouting, "I hate you! I hate you! I hate you!"

UNUTTERABLE LOVE

Ken Abraham

*If we confess our sins, he is faithful and just to forgive us our sins,
and to cleanse us from all unrighteousness.*

1 JOHN 1:9

The grand privilege and obligation of a Christian is that Christ can fill your heart so full of His holy love, you won't be able to contain it all.

While reading these words of Jesus to Martha, "I am the resurrection, and the life: he that believeth in me, though he were dead, yet shall he live: And whosoever liveth and believeth in me shall never die" (John 11:25–26)—instantly my heart was melted like wax before fire; Jesus Christ was revealed to my spiritual consciousness, revealed in me, and my soul was filled with unutterable love. I walked in a heaven of love. Then one day, with amazement, I said to a friend, 'This is the perfect love about which the apostle John wrote, but it is beyond all I dreamed of. In it is personality. This love thinks, wills, talks with me, corrects me, instructs and teaches me. And then I knew that God the Holy Ghost was in this love and this love was God, for 'God is love.'"

LEARNING LOVE

Henry Drummond

God is love. Whoever lives in love
lives in God, and God in them.

1 JOHN 4:16 NIV

That is the supreme work to which we need to address
ourselves in this world, to learn Love. Is life not full of
opportunities for learning Love? Every man and woman
every day has a thousand of them. The world is not a
playground; it is a schoolroom. Life is not a holiday but
an education. And the one eternal lesson for us all is how
better we can love. What makes a man a good cricketer?
Practice. What makes a man a good artist, a good
sculptor, a good musician? Practice. What makes a man
a good linguist, a good stenographer? Practice. What
makes a man a good man? Practice. Nothing else.

We do not get the soul in different ways, under
different laws, from those in which we get the body and
the mind. If a man does not exercise his arm, he develops
no biceps muscle; and if a man does not exercise his
soul, he acquires no muscles in his soul, no strength
of character, no vigor of a moral fiber, nor beauty of
spiritual growth. Love is not a thing of enthusiastic
emotion. It is a rich, strong, manly, vigorous expression
of the whole round Christian character—the Christ-like
nature in its fullest development. And the constituents
of this great character are only to be built up by ceaseless
practice.

TREASURES OF THE HEART

Brother Lawrence

For where your treasure is,
there will your heart be also.

LUKE 12:34

*W*e cannot escape the dangers which abound in life without the actual and continual help of God. Let us then pray to Him for it continually. How can we pray to Him without being with Him? How can we be with Him but in thinking of Him often? And how can we often think of Him but by a holy habit which we should form of it? You will tell me that I am always saying the same thing. It is true, for this is the best and easiest method I know; and as I use no other, I advise all the world to do it. We must know before we can love. In order to know God, we must often think of Him; and when we come to love Him, we shall also think of Him often, for our heart will be with our treasure. This is an argument which well deserves your consideration.

THE FRESH EYE

John Henry Jowett

His compassions fail not.
They are new every morning.

LAMENTATIONS 3:22–23

*W*e have not to live on yesterday's manna; we can
gather it fresh today. Compassion becomes stale when
it becomes thoughtless. It is new thoughts that keep
our pity strong. If our perception of need can remain
vivid, as vivid as though we had never seen it before,
our sympathies will never fail. The fresh eye ensures the
sensitive heart. And our God's compassions are so new
because He never becomes accustomed to our need.
He always sees it with an eye that is never dulled by
the commonplace; He never becomes blind with much
seeing! We can look at a thing so often that we cease to
see it. God always sees a thing as though He were seeing
it for the first time. "Thou, God, seest me," and "His
compassions fail not."

And if my compassions are to be like a river that
never knows drought, I must cultivate a freshness of
sight. The horrible can lose its horrors. The daily tragedy
can become the daily commonplace. My neighbor's
needs can become as familiar as my furniture, and I may
never see either the one or the other. And therefore must
I ask the Lord for the daily gift of discerning eyes, "Lord,
that I may receive my sight." And with an always newly
awakened interest may I reveal "the compassions of the
Lord"!

Beautiful Discoveries

St. Augustine

*O the depth of the riches both of the wisdom and knowledge of God!
how unsearchable are his judgments, and his ways past finding out!*

ROMANS 11:33

*N*ot with doubting but with assured consciousness do I love Thee, Lord. Thou has stricken my heart with Thy word, and I loved Thee. But more deeply wilt Thou have mercy on whom Thou wilt have mercy and wilt have compassion on whom Thou hast had compassion, else in deaf ears do the heaven and the earth speak Thy praises. But what do I love when I love Thee? Not beauty of bodies, nor the fair harmony of time, nor the brightness of the light, so gladsome to our eyes, nor sweet melodies of varied songs, nor the fragrant smell of flowers and ointments and spices, not manna and honey, not limbs acceptable to embracements of flesh. None of these I love when I love my God; and yet I love a kind of light and melody and fragrance and meat and embracement when I love my God, the light, melody, fragrance, meat, embracement of my inner man: There shineth unto my soul what space cannot contain and there soundeth what time beareth not away, and there smelleth what breathing desperseth not, and there tasteth what eating diminisheth not. This is it which I love when I love my God.

A LOVING SPIRIT

D. L. Moody

*"By this everyone will know that you
are my disciples, if you love one another."*

JOHN 13:35 NIV

*I*n the late Professor Drummond's *The Greatest Thing
in the World*, he tells of meeting with natives in the
interior of Africa who remembered David Livingstone.
They could not understand a word he uttered, but they
recognized the universal language of love through which
he appealed to them. It had been many years since
that Christian hero had passed their way, but the very
remembrance of his presence among them would kindle
a friendly smile.

It is this very selfsame universal language of love,
divine, Christlike love, that we must have if we are going
to be used of God. The world does not understand
theology or dogma, but it understands love and
sympathy. A loving act may be more powerful and far
reaching than the most eloquent sermon.

Through Him
That Loved Us

Mrs. Charles E. Cowman

We are more than conquerors
through him that loved us.

ROMANS 8:37

It is better that we should not sing of sadness. There are sad notes enough already in the world's air. We should sing of cheer, of joy, of hope. We do not need to be defeated in our battles, to sink under our loads, to be crushed beneath our sorrows. We may be victorious. Sorrow comes into every life; we cannot shut it away, but we can be conquerors in it. When the snow melts away in the springtime, I have often seen under it sweet flowers in bloom. The very drifts are like warm blankets to keep them safe. So it is with sorrow: Under the cold snows of grief the flowers of the Christian graces grow unhurt. We can overcome in sorrow. This does not mean that we should not shed tears. The love of Christ does not harden the heart; it really makes it more sensitive. The grace of Christ does not save us from suffering in bereavement; yet we are to be conquerors. Our sorrow must not crush us; we must go through it victoriously, with sweet submission and joyous confidence. Let us keep in mind that it is "through Him that loved us."

His Loving-Kindness

Charles H. Spurgeon

"I have drawn you with unfailing kindness."
JEREMIAH 31:3 NIV

The thunders of the laws and the terrors of judgment are all used to bring us to Christ, but the final victory is effected by loving-kindness. The prodigal son set out to his father's house from a sense of need, but his father saw him a great way off and ran to meet him so that the last steps he took towards his father's house were with the kiss still warm upon his cheek and the welcome still musical in his ears.

The Master came one night to the door and knocked with the iron hand of the law; the door shook and trembled upon its hinges, but the man piled every piece of furniture which he could find against the door, for he said, "I will not admit the man." The Master turned away, but by-and-by He came back, and with His own soft hand, using most that part where the nail had penetrated, He knocked again. This time the door did not shake, but, strange to say, it opened, and there upon his knees the once unwilling host was found rejoicing to receive his guest. "Come in, come in. I could not think of thy pierced hand leaving its blood-mark on my door and of thy going away houseless, 'Thy head filled with dew, and thy locks with the drops of the night.'" So in every case; loving-kindness wins the day.

THE PATHETIC MULTITUDE

John Henry Jowett

I have compassion on the multitude, because they have now been with me three days, and have nothing to eat: And if I send them away fasting to their own houses, they will faint by the way: for divers of them came from far.

MARK 8:2–3

My Lord has "compassion upon the multitude." And (shall I reverently say it?) His compassion was part of His passion. His pity was always costly. It culminated upon Calvary, but it was bleeding all along the road! It was a fellow-feeling with all the pangs and sorrows of the race.

And the multitude is round about us still, and the people are in peril of fainting by the way. There is the multitude of misfortune, the children of disadvantage, who never seem to have come to their own. And there is the multitude of outcasts, the vast army of publicans and sinners. And there are the bewildering multitudes of Africa and India and China, and they have nothing to eat!

How do I regard them? Do I share the compassion of the Lord? Do I exercise a sensitive and sanctified imagination and enter somewhat into the pangs of their cravings? My Lord calls for my help. "How many loaves have ye?" Bring out all you have! Consecrate your entire resources! Put your all upon the altar of sacrifice!" And in reply to the call, can I humbly and trustfully say, "O, Lamb of God, I come!"

DAILY CLEANSING

Charles H. Spurgeon

He. . .began to wash his disciples' feet.
JOHN 13:5 NIV

The Lord Jesus loves His people so much that every day He is still doing for them much that is analogous to washing their soiled feet. Their poorest actions He accepts; their deepest sorrow He feels; their slenderest wish He hears; and their every transgression He forgives. Humbly, patiently, He yet goes about among His people with the basin and the towel. He does this when He puts away from us day by day our constant infirmities and sins. Last night when you bowed the knee, you mournfully confessed that much of your conduct was not worthy of your profession, and even tonight you must mourn afresh that you have fallen again into the selfsame folly and sin from which special grace delivered you long ago; and yet Jesus will have great patience with you; He will hear your confession of sin; He will say, "I will, be thou clean;" He will again apply the blood of sprinkling and speak peace to your conscience and remove every spot. It is a great act of eternal love when Christ once for all absolves the sinner and puts him into the family of God; but what condescending patience there is when the Savior with much long-suffering bears the oft recurring follies of His wayward disciple, day by day and hour by hour, washing away the multiplied transgressions of His erring but yet beloved child!